C000177304

Haunted by Waters

Haunted by Waters

A Journey into the Irish Countryside

DAIRE WHELAN

HACHETTE
BOOKS
IRELAND

ATLANTIC
OCEAN

SEA TROUT

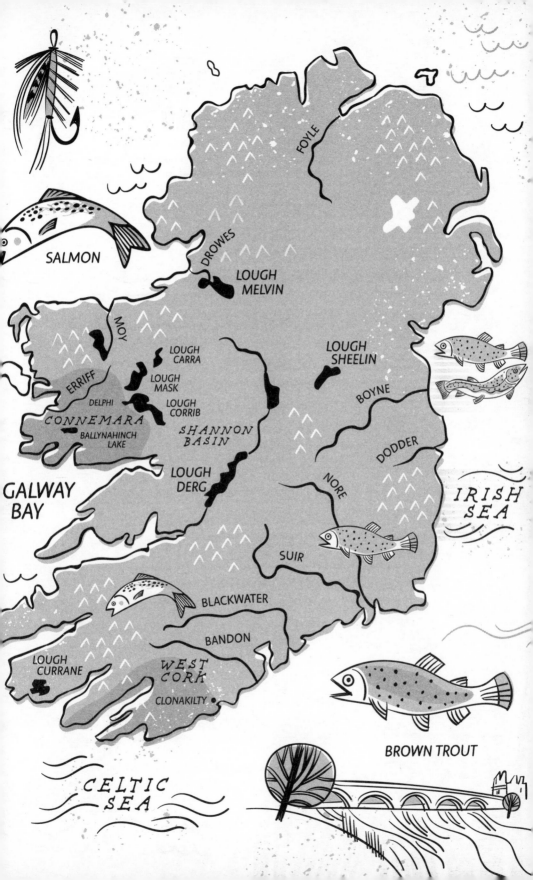

SALMON

FOYLE

DROWES

LOUGH MELVIN

MOY

LOUGH CARRA

LOUGH MASK

ERRIFF

DELPHI

CONNEMARA

LOUGH CORRIB

BALLYNAHINCH LAKE

SHANNON BASIN

LOUGH SHEELIN

BOYNE

DODDER

NORE

LOUGH DERG

GALWAY BAY

IRISH SEA

SUIR

BLACKWATER

BANDON

LOUGH CURRANE

WEST CORK

CLONAKILTY

CELTIC SEA

BROWN TROUT

Copyright © 2021 Daire Whelan

The right of Daire Whelan to be identified as the Author of
the Work has been asserted by him in accordance with the
Copyright, Designs and Patents Act 1988.

First published in Ireland in 2021 by
HACHETTE BOOKS IRELAND

1

All rights reserved. No part of this publication may be reproduced, stored in
a retrieval system, or transmitted, in any form or by any means without the
prior written permission of the publisher, nor be otherwise circulated in any
form of binding or cover other than that in which it is published and without
a similar condition being imposed on the subsequent purchaser.

Cataloguing in Publication Data is available from the British Library

ISBN 9781529388831

Excerpt from 'In the Beginning' by Paul Kingsnorth, from *Songs from
the Blue River* (2018) used with permission by Salmon Poetry

Typeset in Garamond

Book Design and typesetting by Anú Design, Tara
Printed and bound in Great Britain by Clays Ltd, Elcograf S.p.A.

Hachette Books Ireland policy is to use papers that are natural, renewable
and recyclable products and made from wood grown in sustainable forests.
The logging and manufacturing processes are expected to conform to the
environmental regulations of the country of origin.

Hachette Books Ireland
8 Castlecourt Centre
Castleknock
Dublin 15, Ireland

A division of Hachette UK Ltd
Carmelite House, 50 Victoria Embankment, London EC4Y 0DZ

www.hachettebooksireland.ie

For Gloria,
for her own heroic strength of journey.

and this echoing world
and all of its rhythms
will be theirs.

And the girl said, theirs?
But they are so small
and they make straight lines.
How will they manage?

And her father said only:
they will have to.

'In the Beginning', Paul Kingsnorth

Contents

Prologue

I'd returned from three hours of salmon fishing on the Blackwater; fishless – not unusual in itself when fishing for salmon, especially when it's a snatched hour or two where possible – but buoyant and energised again after a few weeks away from the water.

The water level had been ideal for the fly – 0.4m on the gauge – and the conditions were benign, though the warmth in the May sunshine belied a thinness in the air whenever the sun went behind the clouds. For some strange reason, I hadn't even felt much like fishing as I drove down the motorway heading for the exit to Fermoy-Kilworth. It was a Sunday morning, I had a few hours to myself while Trina, my wife, had the kids, so what was there to be complaining about?

I like to think there's a certain apprehension every angler feels as they approach a river. It's the apprehension of wondering how many other anglers will be on the water. How busy will it be? How will I fit in? Nine times out of ten of course these questions are dispelled within minutes. There's never as many as you think, 90 per cent of them are accommodating and friendly, and you always end up having a good time anyway.

It was to be no different this time as I drove down the roadway for the Upper Kilmurry beat on the Blackwater. Four anglers were downstream, I was told, and I could head upstream where I'd have the beat to myself until lunchtime. It was more than I could have hoped for on a May bank holiday weekend. Yes, maybe there hadn't been enough rain recently, but I'd rather the fly landing level on the water than struggling on overflowing banks.

After two hours working my way downstream from the top of the beat, I still hadn't touched or even seen a fish. Despite the low water conditions, I had to be careful where I waded – there were always dangerous pots and holes lurking somewhere – but I was casting a good line out, even though it had been a month since my last outing.

As I made my way downstream, I came to a run that I had only really spun for before in high water from the bank. It was wide, the Blackwater – double-handed wide – but smooth, and the water was only up to my knees. In short, it was perfect fly water. I could wade out a third of the way and have plenty of room for my back-cast.

As I cast and moved, cast and moved, I looked around me. Downstream as far as the steeply curved Lug Pool and back upstream to the Hut Pool, there wasn't a single person to be seen. For as far as I could see, I was the only person on the river. I felt so at home, at peace and contented, I wanted to grab hold of these minutes for eternity.

I could feel my body relax and my casting become smoother, more powerful, more in touch. The line shot out easier and with every cast I felt confident about hitting it right. I was in the zone. Whether the fish were also in the mood I wasn't so sure about, but in mid-stream and with the fly landing straight and fishing right away, I had as good a chance as any.

I watched the line come around from its initial landing, a steady pace following through to the centre of the flow (any minute now …) before reaching the dangle at the near bank and short strips to bring the line in. The sun was out, the water was lapping around my knees and I was casting with an ease and power I couldn't remember having before. The expanse of the Blackwater was before me for a good half a kilometre; I was in the river, on the river and felt part of the river with each cast I made.

I thought to myself, 'When I die and go to heaven this is what it will be like,' as I followed the line out before readying myself for another confident cast. There was no salmon showing or even plucking at my fly, but it didn't really matter. I was in the moment with the beauty and peace of the river that surrounded and flowed around me as I stood there under the sun in solitude. I breathed it all in deeply, wanting to hold it inside me for as long as possible.

No salmon took my fly, and soon I was climbing the ladder out of the river, heading back to the car to change out of my waders and head home. Yet despite the lack of fish, it felt right, I had left on a high. The 'last casts' flew out from my hands and swam perfectly through the water. Fish or no fish, there was nothing more I could have done. There was even a smile I think as I walked back to the car.

Later that day I showed my wife the photos I'd taken on my phone and tried to describe to her the feeling of bliss and perfection I experienced just standing there in the water, the thought I had about being in heaven.

'If I knew that to get to heaven, all I had to do was drive down the road, I'd be going there whenever I could,' she said.

She was right of course. To be so close to something that touches us so deeply, to have it within our grasp and not do anything about it, or only do something when we're at our limit, seems incomprehensible. Earlier that day as I left my house, going fishing for a few hours felt like a drudge and a struggle, but three hours later I found myself elevated and rejuvenated. Such is the power of flowing waters. As Norman Maclean wrote in *A River Runs Through It*, 'I am haunted by waters', and it's what I want inscribed on my gravestone when my turn is up.

Just a year later when the pandemic struck, it was all taken away so quickly and so easily. Something taken for granted and cherished was now out of reach behind lock and key. It was only then that you appreciated what it meant being able to fish, to stand there in the river.

The first lockdown in spring had brought with it a resolve to hunker down and get through the two months or so of sacrifice. After just a few weeks of staying at home, juggling remote working with minding the kids, only venturing out to the supermarket when necessary as well as the nearby woods, the curve, we were told, had been flattened.

But when the summer and autumn brought a resurgence in the pandemic and the lockdown came again in October, there wasn't much to look forward to. There would be no winter sun to escape the claustrophobia to, only rising infections and hospital case-loads.

Up until then Covid-19 was something that happened in the news, in the big cities or somewhere foreign. In rural Ireland you

Haunted by Waters

only read about it. But when someone we knew contracted it and the spread of infection amongst their friends became apparent, it suddenly hit home. In the valley of the mountains between the farms and the fields, Covid was in the air.

We have all passed through the eye of a storm: some have gone closer to it than others, and some have lost their lives. The figures are staggering and numbing at the same time. Death and sickness everywhere. But with vaccines being rolled out, the light at the end of the tunnel is getting brighter – 'hope springs eternal' as they say.

While I waited, nature was my salve and my balm. I ventured out to the nearby woods and stood looking up to the towering yews and conifers, inhaling, exhaling, inhaling, exhaling. My kids thought I was trying to talk to the trees but no, I told them, I'm trying to listen. To listen to what they had to say.

'Don't forget,' I think I heard the trees whisper. 'Let go but never forget this time, of the people lost, the sickness untold, but also the humanity and the coming together.' I inhaled once more before walking on up the path with my kids. I could hear the river rushing downhill on the other side of a copse of small trees.

The sound of running water is the sound of promise and I made my way with the kids through the trees to a small bank of stones and sand beside the water's edge. Even the youngest, Gloria, aged three, was delighted at the sight of the water and soon the three of them were splashing, climbing, throwing, and peering under stones.

I let the sounds of the river wash over my senses and drank it all in. This was rejuvenation and clarity, all brought together here beside this flowing ravine surrounded by the Galtee Mountains. I see the peaks of these mountains every day from the front of our home, they are distant but constant, the edge of the frame to our daily lives. Here is where they call the Golden Vale. On one side the Knockmealdowns look down with the cut of the Vee in their centre – a gap between the mountains takes you to Waterford. Opposite, looming down, is the peak of Galtee Mór with its smaller sisters and brothers, said to look like harps from Celtic mythology. The long range of the Galtees dominates the landscape and the valley upon which lies a patchwork of rich farmland with cows and crops spreads out for as far as the eye can see. To the south and east are the Comeraghs, and Slievenamon standing out on its own, a sentry on Tipperary's border.

Later that day I take another walk, this time by myself, to go around the garden and look down into the valley we had been in earlier. The sun was setting now, the rich orange from her glow lighting up the land before me, and I am reminded not just of days setting but also the inexorable decline of us all.

Covid has merely brought it more sharply into focus these last few months, shining a light on what needed most tending to. Not the treadmill of commute-work-home, but the chance to stand, stop and listen.

I think of the thousands dead in Ireland, the hundreds of thousands in Europe and the millions around the world. And I think of those who died pre-Covid; it is all the one, I ponder, death in a pandemic, death outside of it. The sun still setting and the river still running.

Legacy. That is what I hear when standing still in my garden.

That is what falls upon me in this valley. The legacy of those passed on. Not to be written about in newspaper obituaries or fawning columns, but carried by those whose lives we come to touch every day.

'What you leave behind is not what is engraved in stone monuments, but what is woven into the lives of others,' said Pericles, the Ancient Greek statesman, and I think of what myself and my wife have woven into our kids' lives during their short years so far – their love of running in the woods and fields and splashing in the river; my wife pointing out the bees and birds flitting around the garden; their joy and fascination as I show them fish swimming under the bridge in the town.

The first time I took the boys fishing was two years earlier when they were six and four and it was the unlikeliest of settings: – Prospect Park in Brooklyn, New York City, with high-rise apartment blocks and subways rumbling underground.

But as soon as we walked through the gates to the park and stood by the side of the large, artificial lake, the bustle of the city melted away. We had been living for the last two months in a brownstone in the suburbs of Brooklyn while Trina worked on a research project for New York University.

It was a trip of a lifetime – stressful, hectic and busy but so enriching and rewarding at the same time, to be able to live such a different life if only for a few months. And as kids do, they just fit right in. For country kids who had never been on a train or bus in their lives, hopping on the subway to visit Manhattan became as natural as walking out the front door into fields of corn.

Suburban living in Brooklyn was so different, so multicultural, so all-embracing, yet soon I found myself aching for some fishing and the outdoors as well. I discovered that Brooklyn has its very own Central Park, called Prospect Park, hundreds of acres of green space in the middle of New York's biggest suburban landscape. And there was a fly fishing guide who offered days on the lake with a chance to catch bluegills and the occasional bass on the fly.

Two subway journeys and one platform change later, myself and my two boys arrived in expectant hope by the lakeside where we met Pete, our guide for a few hours' fishing. The boys were squealing with excitement as they saw dozens of fish swimming close to the water's edge before us.

I rigged up with a 3-weight fly rod and, with a mix of small poppers and streamers, cast out into the clear waters. With pretty much every other cast we were catching small bluegills and the routine would be the same. I'd cast out and hand the rod to one or other of my boys. As they stripped the line in slowly, the shadows of the fish could be seen circling, chasing, inspecting the fly before one would engulf it and was hooked.

I'll never forget the sheer jubilation, excitement and absolute wonder as Ryan and Charlie landed their first fish on the fly. As the small bluegill lay flapping on the bank they wanted to touch it, stroke it and care for it as they would any other creature. But they knew we had to put the fish back and they were happy to hold it for a quick picture – with smiles as wide as I've ever seen – before releasing it and watching it swim back to its family and friends. The pictures from that afternoon are still on my phone,

a reminder of just how much their first fishing trip meant to them.

We never had the chance to fish in Prospect Park again and after two months our stay in America was up and it was time to head back to Ireland. We all settled back quickly into our routines of work, school and weekends and though we often spoke about Brooklyn and had the 'remember when' moments, it was becoming more and more distant.

With fishing magazines and fly fishing tackle lying around the house, my boys would be constantly asking me to go fishing again. 'When the weather improves,' I would tell them; 'When the summer comes,' I would say when asked again.

But 2020 arrived and we hadn't ventured out fishing together since that day in Brooklyn which now seemed so very long ago. I made a promise to them, and to myself, that we would do it but then Covid arrived and the lockdowns with it.

So instead we took to parks, woodlands and walking by rivers and I tried to instil in them that same sense of wonder and awe that they first experienced in Prospect Park. They might look at me funny when I stand underneath the tall boughs of the trees breathing in deeply, or when I am lost for minutes staring into the flowing waters of a river, but I think, at the same time, they also know why it is I do it.

The passing of time has become more focused this past year, a sharp lens highlighting to anyone that will listen how little time any one of us really has. It's a time for remembering but also for building legacies, moments and experiences that will never be forgotten.

My boys still ask me, 'When can we go fishing again?'

And I tell them, 'Soon, very soon.'

'When the coronavirus is gone, is it?'

'Yes, when it's gone.'

'And me? I come too?' pipes up three-year-old Gloria, the smallest, not wanting to be left out.

'All of us,' I say with a smile. 'All of us together.'

Introduction

It was a Friday in November in the city. The orange and white streetlights cast a glow in the oily dark. The rain was falling cold and wet on the shoppers who were getting ready for Christmas, judging by their bursting bags. Cars, bumper to bumper on the roads, crawled forward a few inches before stopping and waiting, stopping and waiting. I held onto the handrail on the Luas heading for Heuston station crammed into the carriage with dozens of others. Puddles of rain collected near the doors while the steam from breathless workers who shoved themselves into any tiny space left on the tram rose up through the crowd. As the Luas moved away from the platform the mass of our bodies bumped and swayed against each other on the jolting journey.

I squeezed my hand into my jeans pocket and managed to pull my phone out to check the time. The Dublin to Cork train was due to leave in ten minutes and the Luas still had one more stop. It would take six minutes before I could finally push off the tram and make a dash through the crowded station. It would be close but I had the timings down to the second, a routine all too familiar. My tickets were in my hand waiting as the Luas slowly pulled up and the doors opened. Myself and half a dozen others hurried across the tram lines, all desperate not to miss the train.

I could hear the announcer's voice over the tannoy in the main concourse of the station calling out its imminent departure. Miss this train and there wouldn't be another one for an hour but it was the difference between seeing my kids before they went to bed and reading them a story, kissing them goodnight, or arriving home to a silent house and only seeing them curled up asleep. I pulled the straps of my laptop bag tighter against my shoulder and started into a sprint.

That night I did make it home on time. Panting and out of breath, the doors closed behind me as I jumped on the train packed with workers and students heading home for the weekend. I found a seat and slumped into it, exhausted from the panicked run and a long week of work. I could feel my socks wet from the rain-soaked footpaths and my shirt sticking to my shoulders, sweaty from the dash to make it here. The other three passengers seated around the table looked as wet and miserable as I did. I took out my laptop to get some work finished and not for the first time thought to myself, there has to be something better than this.

That night after stories had been read and the kids tucked into bed, I sat down in my reading chair with a glass of wine. The rain was still falling but it was a comfort to sit and hear it outside splattering against the windows while the fire blazed in front of me. I had two whole days at home to look forward to, two days with my family when I wouldn't be travelling from Tipperary to Dublin. I tried not to think about Monday too much when it would all begin again with a 5 a.m. start in the cold and dark. Instead, I looked up at my books, shelves of non-fiction and fiction writing that gave me the most comfort. One row I found myself being drawn to more and more, the one that I seemed to be adding to the most in recent years. Titles such as *A Man May Fish*, *An Angler for All Seasons*, *Beneath the Black Water* and *I Know a Good Place* were all evocative and alluring, hinting at a world that had become my escape.

I'd describe myself as a fly fisherman who dreams and reads more about fishing than I can actually be on the water; I'm not one of those anglers whose very essence craves to be fishing day in, day out.

Still, it's always been there, that aching love of the water and of catching fish. In stereotypical fashion, I can't go near a river without craning my neck to look and see what lies below. Like any fisherman, I can't explain it, the mystery and allure of fish in waters, having to stop at any bridge and peer down, if only for a few seconds; the holidays and journeys around fishing and wondering about certain fish and certain waters.

The depths of a lake, a river running, or the lapping tides take me to a world of imagining and delight, a world so beautiful and at peace that I am constantly reminded of my own personal turmoil: of the highs and lows of life, trying to find my way, of wondering about my career, the decisions I made along the way, asking if where I am is where I want to be. In contrast, the flowing waters seem to say to me: *Stand here and be still in this moment, just this moment.*

I was introduced to fishing by my aunt's then-husband, a fun-loving character who, despite his outgoing, sociable nature, loved nothing better than getting away from people and city life for a few days of coarse fishing beside a lake or canal.

I was in my early teens and he would regularly bring me and his two boys fishing with him. He was always happy to bring us out and introduce us to the rudiments of float fishing for roach, rudd and tench, showing us how to set up the line with a float, hook and some live maggots squirming on the end.

Casting out, the hook would sink down with the float poking its head above the water. 'Now strike when that float goes under,' he told me. 'That's when your fish is on.'

After the first experience of landing a small roach, I was smitten. Being out in nature, beside the stillness and serenity of the water, aligned with the challenge of catching a fish, brought me a peace as a teenager that I didn't get anywhere else. Maybe that's why I was invited along. Maybe I needed it, maybe it was good for me. And it was.

Growing up in the north Dublin suburbs, the nearest canal or lake fishing was an hour's drive away and nowhere near public transport, so my fishing trips were limited, rare moments of escape. Those summer days when I was brought along were bliss – there was more time in the late, bright evenings to get away and the call would come through from my uncle: 'Do you fancy going fishing next week?' I'd count down the days, get my gear ready and have the lunch made and flask prepared days in advance.

Those summer days as a teenager were a mixed affair. Some memories are happy ones, mainly the younger, more innocent ones, where you didn't feel the pressure of having to 'hang out' in the fields of the housing estate seeing what trouble the gangs would get up to that day. In your mid-teens, if you didn't want in, then you would be cooped up in the house, staring at the walls, while your mother worried about why you were staying in all the time. If only there was fishing nearby, I wanted to tell her, or wild places to explore.

Alongside the fishing trips, I would often spend a week in Galway, where my mum's family was from. It was rural, overlooking Oranmore Bay and surrounded only by fields, cows and occasional houses. Even in my college days I still made weekend trips down to visit my grand-aunt, Maureen, where she would always have the kettle on the boil and a ham sandwich ready. I can still smell the Aga in the small, main room and remember sinking into the soft armchair beside it for warmth. The only sound breaking the silence was the ticking clock on the wall behind me, and sitting there in Curragrean I could relax, read and be a million miles away from life. Whenever I wanted to get away from it all, I knew Galway was waiting for me, and getting onto the Nestor's coach on the Dublin quays on a Friday evening was a deeply satisfying feeling.

The Dublin–Galway railway line passed by the front field of Maureen's cottage and we were taught from a young age how to read the line signal. This was just a small boreen with only five or six houses and no gates to block access across the tracks. Anyone could drive or walk across it, all you had to do was look down the line to the signal box and if it was pointing down then you knew a train was coming. You might still risk it but there were enough stories of near misses and fatalities to know that it wasn't worth it.

The boundaries of our play were as far as the railway line and no further. There were enough fields, rocks and ruins this side of the tracks anyway, but we were often just as happy leaning on the field gate feeling the whoosh and vibrations of an oncoming train, its noise and speed overpowering our eyes and ears as it flew by.

That was Galway, the countryside, far away from Dublin and one of my most treasured places to be. Even during my college years, when parties and socialising became a priority, I relished escaping for weekends at a time just to be down there again, to sit in the old tree in the garden and look out onto the bay once more.

You're never too old for nature and the outdoors, I discovered. I may not have been fishing when in Galway, but being surrounded by the countryside was enough to keep my soul sustained. Fishing was to become one more extension of that.

Was it merely coincidence then that I ended up living in south Tipperary on a farm fourteen years ago, surrounded by fields and mountains, married to a local woman whose summer childhood memories were of playing in the fields surrounding her house, or amongst the haystacks and farm sheds?

We moved down from Dublin having got sick and tired of chasing our tails in the city. We were driving down to Tipp after work on a Friday most weekends and after two years of it, we decided to take the leap and give country living a shot – although I still had to be in Dublin a few times a week for work.

A river flowed near the farm – not just any river, but one of Ireland's mightiest, famed for its fly fishing, the majestic Suir. The third-longest river in Ireland, it rises in the Devil's Bit in north Tipperary before flowing for 115 miles through the south of the county and into Waterford where it meets the sea. Ireland's largest

salmon was caught upstream at Holycross in the nineteenth century but it's the brown trout that it's most famous for – wily, fast fish that have an abundance of fly life to choose from and are not easily fooled by an angler's creation thrown at them.

There are no anglers in my wife's family – in fact, it was difficult to locate many anglers locally; it's a curious fact that so few people who live near rivers or lakes take any interest in fishing.

There was also a golf course about the same distance from the house and most of my friends in Dublin played the game, often going to Scotland or England at weekends to play a few rounds. Golf is one of those great networking skills to have, but although I've played pretty much every sport going, and dabbled in pitch and putt as a teenager, golf never really gripped my imagination. The staid, upper-crust scene of the clubhouse reminded me a bit too much of my school years and I always backed away.

Besides, I knew I would only have time for one all-consuming passion down here: was it going to be fly fishing or golf? If I was going to take up one I knew it would occupy most of my waking hours and everything else in between. I thought back to my happiest memories on the canal or lake, a heaving tench on the end of the line or a bag full of roach in the keepnet at day's end.

The picture of me as a ten-year-old boy wearing a big, beaming smile while holding a decent-sized tench summed up where my heart lay. Golf would have to come in another life. My mind was made up, fly fishing it was. At thirty years of age, this would be my new passion and I would call the River Suir home.

I remember clearly the first few months and years after moving to Tipperary in 2007 when I devoured every fly fishing magazine, article and book going. I couldn't make head nor tail of a lot of it but I knew, eventually, by some form of osmosis, it would all sink in and start to make sense. I was just a holding bay for all this new information and someday soon (I was hoping) it would be downloaded and processed for suitable use.

I threw myself into the culture of fly fishing, confident I was on the right path. I started reaching out to guides and instructors and began to get to know a group of experts that I knew I could call upon for many years to come and they accepted me completely into the world that dominated their lives. I was only an interloper, but happy to be allowed to join in the conversations.

I still didn't know much and my interactions could be stilted and awkward, using the wrong phrase, terminology or language, but I was slowly finding my feet. At least I could start to sound like a fly fisherman, if not quite fish like one.

I'll never forget my first foray to the Suir. Tom, a neighbour from across the fields who liked to venture out fishing on a summer evening, knew I had begun to take an interest and offered to take me down to the river for an evening's rise to give me a taste of what it was all about.

He even came with a rigged-up rod for a spot of bubble float fishing with a cast of two wet flies and a float on top. 'Cast out and let the line come around downstream as you reel in slowly,' he told me. 'Strike firmly as soon as you see the bubble dipping.' Simple and ingenious, it was a perfect way to introduce someone to brown trout fishing using flies but without the difficult technique of fly casting. I'm not so sure of its legality though and a friend once told me to drop the rod if anyone approached asking me for my licence. 'Run after that,' I was told only half in jest.

It was a perfect balmy August evening as Tom and I headed off in the car after dinner. I was as excited as if I was ten again. We climbed over a gate and walked through pastures up and then downhill before we got to the river. The low sun cast an iridescent golden hue on the sky. Flies were hatching, fish were rising and the land was lulling itself from a summer's day into night. All was perfect in the world.

I cast out with my rod, the bubble float and wet flies expertly tied on for me by Tom landing gently on the water. 'Across and down, reeling slowly in, that's it, you're doing it right,' he reassured me. It was the type of fishing I was used to and it worked a treat. Within minutes I was into my first-ever wild brown trout, a tiny 6-inch specimen of brown-spotted perfection. I unhooked him and watched him dart off into the moving waters.

This was for me, I decided, this was the life I wanted to live, casting into the river with artificial flies to catch trout and salmon under setting summer suns. Does it get any better or more straightforward? I thought to myself, marvelling at the scene around me. Further downstream Tom's father, Joe, was wading far out, the river up to his chest as he expertly cast a long line out. He seemed so in the moment that nothing else mattered. I might have only been fishing bubble and float style this evening but I knew I would be going out the very next day to buy a fly rod to learn to cast. I watched the other anglers around me in awe as they effortlessly cast the line out before them.

I caught a few more trout that evening and I couldn't keep the beaming smile off my face. It's still there in the photo taken back home in the farmhouse kitchen, me grinning as I held the brown trout that I had brought home to show my wife and her parents. If only life could always be so easy.

As my interest in and passion for fly fishing grew over the next ten years, I started to venture further afield, reading about the incredible choice of fisheries right across the country. Not just fishing locations but places of historical interest and influence – some of the wildest, most remote parts of the country where it's just you, a river and the surrounding mountains for company.

But there's only so many days in a year and only so many times one can go fishing. Work and family commitments take up most of my time now so fishing days are precious and planned well in advance, circled in red and looked forward to with excited anticipation, not unlike Christmas when I was a child.

However, if there's one thing I kick myself for it's not going fishing enough. Sometimes it can be too easy to find reasons why it doesn't suit and before you know it you're in the back end of the season staring at too many missed opportunities.

I missed a lot of fishing in 2018 – the usual excuses of too much work, not enough time, finding it too easy at the end of a stressful week to sit in the armchair with a glass of wine and read about fly fishing instead of actually going out – but I was determined to right it the next year.

That rainy Friday evening in November as I sat by the fire looking across at my shelf of fly fishing books, I reached for my notebook and pen and started to make a plan. I knew I couldn't get away from the commuter–work hamster wheel on Mondays but could I start to fish the places around Ireland that I had always wished I could visit? Where could I fish and when? Could I squeeze some working weeks into four days and fit a few free Fridays into my schedule? And with so many fisheries in all the provinces, where to begin?

The salmon season didn't start until 1 January while the trout season began in March, so I still had some time to prepare and plan. As I wrote down the names of the places I would go to, I found the exhaustion of the day slip away and excitement begin to lift my heart once more.

The first destination to decide on at least was easy: 1 January on the River Drowes, the traditional starting point for the fly fishing year. It's a short river – only five miles long – flowing from Lareen Bay on Lough Melvin in County Leitrim before entering the sea at Tullaghan just outside Bundoran in Donegal in the north-west, but it's where the first salmon of the season is regularly caught. After that it was a case of narrowing my list down to regular monthly day trips where possible, to follow the fly fishing season across the country.

The Blackwater is my 'local' salmon river and I always try to be there for its opening in February, likewise the Suir for brown trout in March is just down the road; while further west, Connemara has always held a special place for me, like a spiritual home. My page was beginning to fill up quickly.

Then there's the bass fishing in the summer, I noted, and a unique trip to Dublin and the Dodder that I always wanted to try. As I worked in the capital a few days a week, I loved the thought of bringing my fly rod along with my laptop to work and being able to cast a line out during the day in the city.

At the back end of the season, Lough Currane in Kerry held a special fascination for me, with its October sea trout fishing opportunities. Plus there were the characters and personalities I wanted to meet along the way, ghillies (guides) and fishery owners whose lives had been wrapped up in fly fishing and who had a special perspective on the sport and its people. It may be a cliché but it's true: the people you meet along the way are what make it so enjoyable.

It wasn't a 'best of' or exhaustive list of places to fly fish in Ireland – I just didn't have time for everywhere in one season – but there would be other years, other seasons, and I wanted to make a start somewhere. The other bodies of water – Rivers Moy, Bandon, Boyne, Nore, Finn, Foyle and Erriff; Loughs Sheelin, Derg, Carra and Mask and many more – would still be there waiting for me. The beauty of fly fishing in Ireland is that you're never done – I see myself fishing all around this country until the end of my days in one long stretch of fly fishing nirvana. I finished my list – my own Christmas wish list – and went to bed dreaming of catching fish in wild places.

What follows isn't an account of how to catch salmon, brown trout, sea trout or bass; I'm nowhere near qualified or experienced enough to impart any knowledge. I'm still learning every time I'm on the water and I value the insights and deep knowledge of guides hugely – they make me a better angler every time. It was a year of learning in so many other ways. Of being able to press pause on the working life for part of the time; of taking time out from the busy world not of our making but which we drown ourselves in five days a week; of being able to surround myself

 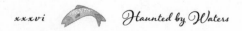

with something more, something bigger. Fly fishing and nature can help soothe the turmoil of life, as I was to discover.

My inconsistent catches as documented throughout the book also point to the fact that I'm not half as successful as I want to be but I also like to think that I'm not alone in that, that there are many more anglers out there like me who curse themselves and the fish for the blank days, tangled tippets, flies caught in trees and lost fish. I won't say those failures are enjoyable but as I have to remind myself when I get frustrated, every day on the water is a learning day: just breathe in, slow down and enjoy being in the privileged position of being on the river or lake.

The striking thing, from fishing in so many places throughout the year and speaking to all the guides and owners, is the one constant refrain: of change, changing times, changing weather, changing fish. The fish numbers are not what they once were, and anglers decry that it's not getting any better. We are all witness to the effects of climate change and there's a growing awareness of how humans are blighting nature, animals and wildlife. Yet knowing what we know and seeing what we're seeing with our own eyes, not enough is being done.

The salmon, which is declining dramatically in numbers, is seen by many as the warning sign for the rest of nature. Their heroic lifecycle means they need clean rivers when they're born before going out to the ocean where they need an abundance of food to grow before returning to spawn in their rivers of birth. Their journey was already fraught with so many dangers and obstacles, yet they always found a way to survive and thrive. But not anymore, it seems.

From pollution and bad water quality in the rivers to fish farms in the estuaries, and over-fishing and warming temperatures in the oceans, salmon are threatened daily as a result of human activity and it is a battle they are losing. And yet still we fish. Still we believe and hope. As long as there are fish to be caught we will still cast a line.

However, it is not just the salmon that are losing, we too are losing out every day that action isn't taken. Scientists, politicians, campaigning groups – even anglers – are all trying to do what's possible but without radical action, without major bold steps to alter our very approach to modern living, then we are only tinkering around the edges. Perhaps it will take something radical to occur, such as major environmental change or major social upheaval, before we as a species will act in the right way.

And then of course one came. A once-in-a-century pandemic that we were all so unprepared for, a world and our lives shut down, and everything put on hold in the race to develop a vaccine to survive.

As I began to write this book chronicling my fly fishing journey in the winter of 2019, recounting my experiences that took me across so much of Ireland, meeting so many people, little did I think that this would all come to an abrupt close in 2020. I had so many plans, so many places I still wanted to see and then it was gone just like that.

I had discovered something else as well. Part of the reason for the journey was to push myself out more, to get off the endless cycle of commute-work-commute-home-bed-repeat that had become non-stop and monotonous. By 2018 I felt I had lost something of myself, somewhere between Thurles and Heuston and the constant to and fro from one to the other. Surely life was about more than work emails, calls and meetings for ten hours a day? Much of my day was on iPhone and laptop screens, sucked into a digital world and cut off from what was around me.

Often as I stood on the platform at Thurles station in the dark and the cold and looked up to see the headlights of the train approaching, I wondered what it would be like if the train was going the other way, not to the city but into the heart of the countryside to the rivers, fields, mountains, lakes and sea; to a place where drudgery, stress and lack of fulfilment would be taken away.

In the winter of 2018 I had decided that the following year would be different, I would venture beyond myself, beyond my introspection and lack of action. I would live life 'out there' in the countryside, in the Ireland I had lost touch with.

I like to think that Covid was a wake-up call for us all. With vaccinations now widely distributed we all want to get back to 'normal life' but then again maybe we shouldn't be too quick to want to do so. The pandemic has shown us how quickly everything can be taken away from us. We were lucky this time. Science was able to find a way.

Covid has taught us what we truly appreciate, from our close ties with our families and friends and our interactions with other people, to being able to travel and visit the wonderful places this world has to offer. Before the pandemic, I got to experience a magical journey in 2019, a journey that showed me what the Irish countryside and people could offer and what was possible once we chose not to be weighed down by the stresses and strains of everyday life. Being brave in leaving it all behind, if only for a day or two here and there, was all that was needed to realign my compass. I had discovered a freshness where things had been stale and I was excited for what the start of the next decade could bring. But then it was all snatched away when the pandemic hit. But I live in hope that my journeys can still continue.

I just want to be able to go there with a fly rod in my hand.

1.
Pilgrim's Journey to the Drowes

*I*t's the end of the Christmas holidays. After all the preparations, Santa toys, friends and gatherings, tonight, on New Year's Eve, I'm driving alone across the country in the darkness, with four hours of road ahead of me. The kids are tucked up in bed and I've kissed my wife goodbye. The car is packed with my rods, reels, flies and an overnight bag. 'See you next year,' I said to her and she smiled, knowing how much this means to me.

I'm doing something that's been in the back of my mind ever since I took up fly fishing, and that's to mark the start of the New Year by wetting a line on the River Drowes in County Leitrim on opening day, 1 January: New Year's Day. It's the traditional start to the fly fishing year in Ireland and the Drowes is one of the first rivers to open where you have a chance of catching the first salmon of the season. The river may be short on its journey from Lough Melvin to the sea but it's iconic and punches above its weight alongside the bigger rivers such as the Blackwater, Nore, Suir and Shannon.

Although only five miles long, the Drowes has long had a place in Irish history. *Drobhaois* is its original Irish name, meaning 'muddy river' from its rain-soaked banks, and it has been the traditional border line between the provinces of Ulster and Connacht, the clear delineation between these two ancient kingdoms.

I'd spoken to other anglers who had made the trek up in the middle of night only to be greeted by biting wind and torrential downpours. 'Never again,' they'd muttered to themselves, sodden and ice-bitten, as they'd trudged home just a few hours later.

This year has been different though. Talking to Florence, the owner of the B&B where I'll be staying, she says the weather has been fine and dry for weeks. People are out walking and enjoying the sunshine, she tells me. The birds have been singing in the morning and there's not a hint of frost on the ground. It's been up to 13 degrees during the day – a far cry from the usual end-of-December conditions.

The year before, we had a few feet of snow in March, a hurricane and four months without rain. Every year brings with it an ever-changing planet and we can all but hold our collective breaths for what will follow. This balmy 31 December is no exception.

There's a loneliness to setting out on your own on New Year's Eve, although, in truth, I'm doing it not just out of adventure, but also as a promise to myself to live more, do more, be more. The last few years, with three kids under six, has been hectic and it becomes all too easy to sit at home with a glass of wine reading about or watching fishing instead of living it. What better way then to start as you mean to go on than with an eight-hour round trip on the opening day of the season?

There's a few hours still to midnight and, as I pass on the road, the pubs are filling up or people are drawing in for the night. The starlit spires of the churches are the few remaining lights set against the hills, and even the garages are shutting early to give everyone a chance to enjoy the last big celebration of the Christmas festival. One final fling of the year before a new one begins.

There's something about Christmas, birth and New Year beginnings. Resolutions, clean slates, starting over – it's all there – and for the angler it's no different. We make a fresh start by clearing out the old flies and old gear and refreshing our tackle and fly boxes for the season to come. We sit down and plan the trips we're going to make.

I drove on through the night, past junction after junction of the motorway into the darkness. I was driving in cruise control trying to keep alert with tea, chocolate and water. Lights from the houses, buildings and cars flashed across the landscape as I sped on by, pondering how the road goes on and on into the darkness, into the night.

After three and a half hours of driving, I had gone from the rich pastures of Tipperary, past Limerick and under the Shannon before the stone walls and rugged fields of Clare and Galway told me I was on the western coast. I continued north, the spire of Tuam Cathedral lit up by Christmas lights in the distance, and on through Mayo. The signs for Belmullet and Achill hinted that the Atlantic wasn't far away, before I arrived in Sligo and got the first sense of the sea with the surf boards outside the shops and the signs for the Wild Atlantic Way dotted along the coast. The Atlantic Ocean was out there in the swelling darkness, and so were the salmon, returning home.

After Sligo I passed through Drumcliff, a typical rural Irish village with a ruined graveyard under the watchful eye of Ben Bulben. You wouldn't give it a second glance if it wasn't the burial place of W.B. Yeats. 'Cast a cold eye / On life, on death / Horseman, pass by' reads Yeats's self-composed epitaph on his gravestone and I said a silent prayer to one of my literary heroes as I drove on.

The closer it gets to midnight, the lonelier it becomes driving on your own. I can picture the kids fast asleep and the house all quiet, Trina in bed watching Netflix and double-checking her phone to see if I've texted yet to say I've arrived. Most New Year's Eves I'd prefer the warmth of my home, but not this year. The road gets quieter and quieter as you go through the towns, fewer and fewer people are on the streets, some in a rush to get somewhere just to be surrounded by other people, not wanting to be alone in the run-up to midnight. Instead I'm making my lone pilgrimage in homage to the salmon. The stillness of the night is perceptible now and the lights shining on the streets seem to cast a darker glow. Nearly there.

I see the signs announcing Bundoran, I'm only a quarter of an hour away now. The car dashboard says it's 23:10 and the first rain showers are coming in off the ocean. The street lights and roundabout announce the outskirts of Bundoran, a Donegal seaside town that is usually heaving during the summer months with surfers and tourists. Between the beaches, restaurants, pubs and the waves it's a town for visitors, but in the off-season on wet December nights all the amusements and rides are closed and only the locals are left. They crowd into their favourite haunts and hope for another good year to come. On the main street, I see people in shirts and dresses hurrying to get in out of the unexpected rainfall.

At the far side of the town I cross over the Drowes at Lennox's Bridge, a narrow single-lane bridge that tells me I'm crossing into Leitrim. But it's too dark to stop and take a look; I can feel my heart begin to beat faster though. I've left the cosy hotels and pubs behind and am back in the countryside. I'm following the path of the river upstream looking for my B&B. Minutes later I cross the Drowes again, this time at the Four Masters Bridge. I stop the car for a moment so I can get out to look, by the light of my phone, at the copper and stone monument overlooking the river.

'Along the banks of this River Drowes in the House of the Friars of Donegal 1632–36,' reads the inscription, 'Brother Michael Ó Clérigh, with his lay associates Peregrine O'Duignan, Leitrim, Peregrine Ó Clérigh, Donegal, and Fearfeasa O'Mulconry, Roscommon, compiled the Annals of the Four Masters, which record the history of Ireland down to AD 1616.'

Five hundred years ago while these same waters flowed by, in a Franciscan friary on the banks of the river four monks busily wrote and compiled their version of Irish history stretching back into the early ages. The Annals are accounts of battles, plagues, the lives and deaths of kings: a record of Ireland taken from earlier, since disappeared accounts. It's a unique window looking back into the centuries of Gaelic chieftains and I'm standing here in a moment of time, connected by the river to the past, feeling an undeniable link to those monks so long ago. I listen to the sounds of the water as it flows over its riverbed and wonder did they stop for a break every now and again to listen like I am doing. Did they even hear a salmon leaping?

A river's real importance was in providing food and it was the monks who deliberately established their monasteries beside the weirs where the fish could be easily caught and harvested. Rivers, and their salmon especially, were important sources of life. I feel the intertwining of nature as the Drowes weaves its way through the land in this part of the country and then I return to my car and drive on down the road.

When I arrive at the B&B the door is unlocked and I knock quietly before going in. The lights are on and almost everyone has gone to bed but I'm shown to my room by Florence, the owner, and I've time for a quick cup of tea and to text Trina to let her know I've arrived safely. 'Happy New Year!' I type out before settling down to sleep, exhausted but excited for the day ahead.

It's 6.53 a.m. and the alarm on my phone quietly buzzes. I jump up and can hear the sizzling pan in the kitchen already where Florence is preparing an Irish fry. As I wait for the rashers and eggs to cook we chat in the kitchen sipping early-morning coffee and she tells me how fewer and fewer anglers are coming to stay.

'It's dying out,' she admits. 'More and more, people are travelling up in the morning and leaving that same evening. Opening day is still huge here and it's great fun to see all these people out in the worst weather conditions. They're pure crazy. I've seen them go out when you wouldn't put a dog out in it, but those that do stay are not staying as long.'

Two more anglers join me at the table as Florence serves the rashers, pudding and fried eggs. We eat in silence, contemplating the day ahead. There's no rush, but I'm the first out the door, keen to get to the fishing office to pick up my salmon licence.

It's a cool morning and there's been a bit of rain overnight.

Driving in the darkness along the driveway to the fishery office I see other anglers up and about already, driving in and out of the estate. The day won't officially start until 8.30 a.m. when the sun is rising and the first streaks of light awaken us to the river's potential.

It's also an open fishery today which means there's no fee and you can come and go as you please to try and catch the first salmon of the season. And as an added bonus, with it being the Year of the Salmon (an awareness campaign to highlight the importance of the Atlantic salmon, set up and run by the North Atlantic Salmon Conservation Organization), there's a bar of silver up for grabs for the first one caught and released.

I park the car outside the old outhouses of the Lareen estate alongside about a dozen other cars and meet Shane Gallagher, the Drowes fishery owner who has been here since 6 a.m. and working hard in the weeks over Christmas making sure everything was ready for 1 January. It's his busiest time of the year but also the most eagerly anticipated.

Shane's family have lived on the banks of the river for hundreds of years, first as mill owners then as fishery owners but it wasn't until 1977, when his father Thomas bought the estate, that they had the right to fish its waters.

'We had owned land around the River Drowes but we hadn't been allowed to fish on the river we grew up on,' he tells me as we meet up in the small office that doubles up as a tackle shop, an Aladdin's den of assorted fishing tackle and photos from days gone by.

While families such as the Gallaghers worked the land around the river for centuries, the fishing rights remained exclusively in the hands of the owner of the estate, a gentleman from Dublin, Luke White, who made his fortune first by selling second-hand newspapers and books and then from lottery sales. White established the Lareen estate accumulating land in the area from 1810 on and building Lareen House in 1822. The estate passed through various hands and families until 1977 when Thomas Gallagher seized the opportunity to buy it and on 1 January 1978 opened the river to the public for the first time. 'My father wanted to try and make salmon fishing accessible to as wide an audience as possible. The passion is just as great no matter how far your pocket can stretch.' Since then it has been a day rich in tradition – about camaraderie, renewing acquaintances and marking the opening of the salmon fishing season in Ireland.

People travel the length and breadth of the country to be here, some through the night, waiting outside the tackle shop for Shane to open the doors at 6 a.m. with a hot tea, coffee or something stronger.

Shane also explained to me why 1 January held a certain poignancy: 'Opening day of the season was bigger than Christmas in our house and it was a huge part of my father's life. He had caught the first salmon himself on a couple of occasions. In 2002, an angler from Enniskillen caught the first fish and brought it in to the tackle shop to get a photograph. My dad got a photograph taken with the fish, went away to wash his hands and died of a massive heart attack on the spot … it's a fitting tribute to him that we keep it going and try to protect the ethos he instilled.'

After graduating from college Shane had intended to work in business, but when his father died he came home sooner than expected and took over the running of the fishery.

'I grew up here and it's all I know really. The water is in my blood. I've three kids now, my sons Thomas and Conor, and daughter Lilly Anne. They're having a childhood similar to my own, growing up beside the river, getting to know the customers and messing around in boats. From a lifestyle point of view it can be very good, though it is very busy during the nine-month season when I would work six and a half days a week, trying to take a half day on Sunday.'

It's just after 7 a.m. and there isn't a hint of cold in the air, the holly in the bushes the only sign of the Christmas season outside. I drive down to Lennox's Bridge, a few miles downstream, tackle up and wait for the starting time along with about twenty other cars. Finally the sun starts to trickle through and I see the boots of cars parked behind me opening up. Time to stretch my legs and test the air.

Waders are pulled on, shirt and fleece jacket tucked snugly underneath, the wading belt fastened tight. On goes a light rain jacket and fishing waistcoat to hold my fly boxes, tippet and leader material is slung on, gloves and hat stuffed into a back pocket.

I've no net though. I found it bent out of shape during an end-of-season gear check and I haven't got around to getting a new and better one. Thinking about it, probably about 80 per cent of my salmon fishing thus far has been without a net, and also fishless. If there's some subconscious correlation there, I'm choosing to ignore it.

My wife tells me, when I return after another blank session, 'It's all in the mind. I'm telling you, if you go out expecting to catch a salmon, you will! It's that simple!'

Trouble is, when a lot of your salmon fishing consists of snatched hours here and there, whenever you can, and not based on optimum river height, rains or runs, then you're going to struggle. I know of an angler who caught more than thirty salmon last season – but then I discovered that he had fished for more than 100 days.

A young family life, work and other commitments mean I'll never see 100 fishing days in a single season, but that's why I read about the fly fishing fanatics and think wistfully about living such a life. Then I look at the clock on my bedside locker and realise it's nearly midnight and I've to be up in five hours' time for the early train to Dublin for work.

But here, this morning, I am living a dream of sorts. I walk across the hard, dry field and join the other anglers walking along the wooden walkways that line the river bank, muttering 'good morning' while peering into the flowing waters of the Drowes, wondering will I be the lucky one today to claim the bar of silver.

I keep walking, wanting to get away from the crowds. This is what I've been trying to get away from: the mass of bodies on streets, roads and trains that I'm used to. I'll trudge for miles if needed, somewhere I can feel like I'm away from it all. Even here in a river in the corner of Leitrim I need to tell myself to slow down and be patient. Today it's more a case of finding a less crowded corner than the others, and knowing the further I walk from the road and the cars, the better chance I have, I keep walking and wondering.

Unbelievably, I'm sweating now. There's even some flies coming off the water in dribs and drabs, such is the mild temperature of the day. I can feel the drops of moisture run down the side of my forehead. I pull off my cap and replace it again, then stop at one particular spot with some space around me and begin to pull line from my rod.

I'm surprised at how narrow the river is – perhaps only thirty feet to the far bank – and my large double-handed rod feels over-gunned and intrusive here. I'm conscious of the bushes and trees behind me and attempt the casts that I can. I watch the slow drag of the flow – as still as a canal in some places – struggling to breathe life into my fly.

Every other cast, it seems, is getting caught in the bankside vegetation. I have to hold the rod up as I walk upstream to the guilty bush and spend another minute extracting the hook from a godforsaken bramble or twig.

As I reach the limits of the lower stretches of the river I come across a perfectly placed rock about waist height and wide enough for two people. Perfect for sitting on, the rock has been smoothed over the years from anglers resting and reflecting there. Time for an early cuppa, I decide.

I've just opened my flask of hot tea, when another angler joins me to take a break. With our two rods resting on either side of us, I offer him a tea.

Brian is his name, he says, from Dungannon, and he's been fishing the Drowes for about forty years, making the 150-mile round trip throughout the season.

'Initially it was with my wife,' he tells me in his relaxed Ulster drawl. 'But when the kids came along it was just myself most of the time.'

He remembers the years gone by when the fishing was so much better. 'But last year I only had two salmon – two! – against the ten or twenty I'd be normally getting. The fish just aren't there. But I love the Drowes and still come every New Year's Day.'

We stare into the river in silence, wondering where all the salmon have gone, as if we can spot them hiding out in the water some place. We wonder out loud about climate change, the environment, fishing practices at sea, survival rates, even mackerel numbers. Change. The conversation is dominated by change – in the world around us, nature, even society and the rural way of life. Dungannon, Brian tells me, has a sizeable population of people from East Timor, South America and countries in Africa. The world has come to rural villages and towns and it's hard to comprehend, he says.

I know what he means about change, though. I live in rural Ireland, outside Cahir in south Tipperary, which also has a meat-processing factory on its outskirts where many employees come from outside of Ireland; an estimated one-third of the town's inhabitants are now people who have moved to Ireland from other places, and talk invariably turns to the changing make-up of towns and villages around the country. Older generations, especially, find it hard to get their heads around the vast changes being experienced on a daily basis – and not just from a multicultural perspective either.

For anglers, and salmon fishers particularly, the environmental changes being experienced are acute as well. It's one thing reading and hearing about climate change, but when its effects are being felt on the end of the fishing rod in front of your face, it's a change that's hard to ignore.

I finish my tea and decide to head back to the car to go upstream again. I wish Brian all the best for the coming season, and all going well, I tell him I might see him on the river next 1 January.

As I make my way back upstream, I throw the occasional line out into the gaps between anglers, and even find a lovely, short run worth wading into, casting below the trees on the far bank. This is better, feeling the cold water running past my legs, the current reminding me of the river's life force and the rod and line curving gracefully from left to right and then across and downstream. Still no sign of a salmon, however, and I reel in.

The other anglers I spoke with had no luck either. People didn't seem to care though – they were out on the water, the day was mild and enjoyable, it wasn't a chore to be fishing today, and I felt like they had finally broken through the dark days of winter.

I drive back to Shane Gallagher's tackle shop and office and the place is buzzing with the chatter of returning anglers. In the kitchen across the yard, rolls and soup are being dished out to the hungry crowd while talk invariably turns to the morning's fishing. No one had caught anything so far this morning and no fresh fish had been seen either, but everyone remained expectant and eager.

'The conditions are perfect' was the common refrain but talk again turned to 'changing conditions' and 'changing times'. The anglers beside me had caught their first salmon in drastically different weather to what we were seeing today – everything from wind and rain to freezing snow and ice.

'The Russian salmon' was also a hot topic of conversation. These were the pink salmon that had begun to appear in Irish rivers in the last few years and were starting to become more common. Farmed in the Kola peninsula, they had escaped and had begun spreading out beyond their Russian waters, even straying as far afield as Ireland's west coast.

We don't know yet if the pink salmon are here to stay but if climate change is a root cause, will future generations be sitting around the fishery on New Year's Day talking about the first pink salmon of the year and how the mighty and legendary Atlantic salmon once ruled the rivers but no more?

It's an apocalyptic vision but, much like the ongoing effects of climate change, perhaps worst-case scenarios are what need to be grasped and acted upon.

I head out again and fish on for a few more hours, parking by the Four Masters Bridge. Everywhere I drive there's cars parked beside the river with rods and rod holders sticking out from the bonnets of many, all coming not in expectancy but maybe with just a sliver of hope.

As I cast out a line on another stretch of water, I meet Dave, a regular angler on the Drowes, who is steadily fishing his fly downstream. Rhythmically and methodically, he pulls in some line, turns and lifts the rod upstream before casting out a majestic length of line. He tells me about his own obsession with salmon. 'Fishing is actually like an illness, it's such an addictive thing and thankfully there's no cure for it. If you get a salmon it's exhilarating and you love it, and if you don't get one you travel the length and breadth of the country to try and get one. It needs to be in your blood ... I've been fishing since I was a young boy and I will continue fishing to the day I drop. I'll probably keel over on a riverbank. A nice way to go anyway.' I nod and know what he means.

Further upstream, a German couple I meet tell me they have been coming to the Drowes since 1999. 'We come here for fly fishing and for the nature; the people they are very friendly and kind. It's so calm and quiet here and we can have a wonderful holiday. We come only to here, and have never been to any other part of Ireland. We have been coming since 1999 but never had a salmon but still we come every year.'

Twenty years fishing and never having caught a salmon? I'd choose a different sport after that amount of time, I think to myself, but I can see the wistful look they have for the river and wish them the best of luck.

It's now early afternoon and still no sign of the elusive salmon. It will be getting dark soon enough. A four-hour drive awaits me and I want to be home in time for the kids' bedtime. A quick call to them at lunchtime assured them that yes I was fishing, but no, there was no fish. A picture of a fish, any fish, they ask me. With the sun setting low across the distant fields, I reel in and return to my car where I pack away my rod and gear. I bid a quiet farewell to the Drowes and drive away with the January sun shining low across the bay.

I leave without a touch or a sign of a salmon but I have marked the start of the season. I have made the journey cross-country and up the coast to pay homage to the first day of the fly fishing year, and I have at least experienced at first-hand what the day means to so many who come more in hope than expectation from every part of Ireland, and beyond.

But, with salmon numbers continuing to fall, how much longer will the hope remain, I wonder.

I often think of something that Noel Carr of the Federation of Irish Salmon and Sea Trout Anglers (FISSTA) told me once about a regular visitor to Ireland's shores.

'There's one particular Spanish guy, from northern Spain, who comes every year,' he explained. 'He flies into Shannon with his wife and two children, starting off with the Galway Weir, then the Moy and finally the Finn in Donegal just to see salmon leaping because it doesn't exist where he's from. This is a living museum in Ireland at the moment, but for how long?'

Shane Gallagher is an optimist though, and maybe we have to be that way, otherwise we wouldn't head out fishing. He believes in nature's ability to fight back.

'Everybody talks about the good old days, but we've had good years and bad years before. Definitely the river produced more fish early on but we've had days with thirty to forty fish caught still and I'd consider that prolific. Back in the 1980s I'd see fish with UDN [ulcerative dermal necrosis, a disease that affects salmon and sea trout] and their dorsal fins torn from nets. You don't see that anymore, the fish are clean as a whistle, not marked and with no spots.'

Just how much do we look back with rose-tinted glasses anyway? It's fascinating to read old catch diaries for the Drowes, and one from 1941 has entries that read:

'Bad season, no floods till end of Sept'

'Total one clean fish in Oct'

'Reasonable fishing day this season'

'Cold and dull, other pools also'

'Very few fish rising'

Sounds all too familiar for the twenty-first century, not just 1941.

'I don't buy into the "you should have been here twenty years ago" talk,' says Shane. 'We're here in the present and have to live with what we have. Yes there are some rivers in a bad state but there's no reason why we can't protect what we have and gradually rebuild it. I would make it my life's work to make sure that wild salmon are running the river when my son is my age now.'

As I head homewards and the minutes and hours pass, the towns and villages begin to come back to life after their New Year's Eve revelries. The rain showers coming in off the Atlantic have cleared and the roads are getting busier.

A snatch of conversation from earlier drifts back to my mind. How one of the anglers in the lunchroom had mentioned that this was the first time he had been out fishing in about two years since his stroke. Only two weeks previously, he said, he wasn't even able to get out of bed or walk around, 'but here I am alive and walking the river again. That's how you know you've recovered, when you're back appreciating nature and all it has to offer'. Alive again to fish, that was what meant the most to him.

It's nearly 7 p.m. when I pull up outside the house. The lights are on upstairs and the kids are getting ready for bed. I'm just in time to read them their stories and tell them about the adventure

I had that day, trying to catch the first salmon of the year. 'Not this time,' I tell them, but their faces still light up as I tell them about the river and its history, the monks, the fishery and all that happened during the day. I'm a pilgrim returned home, having paid my respects to this sacred day, but now it's time for sleep and dreams of what may lie ahead for the coming season.

2.

Faith in the Blackwater

The cold, bleak days of January move slowly on. All this talk of rebirth and beginnings is always short-lived in the first month of the year. Promises made, promises broken. You start off flying on 1 January but by the second week you're struggling to keep up, and by the third you're falling back outside the placings.

You don't mind work, really. It's just that – work – and it's what gets you through. You don't want to think about twenty years hence in case that's all there is. And if you're buying a house, moving house, having a baby, looking after a baby, changing jobs or stuck in your job, chances are you would give anything to just get away from it all – if only for a few hours.

For some it's the football. Fall deeply for a team's fortunes and your own life's ups and downs can be substituted for the team's. It hurts less if it's only the Premier or Champions League results that your mood today is riding on. For others, solace is found in the bottom of a glass of wine or beer.

I've tasted and tried other vices and thankfully come out the other side, seeing a world that could go awry for me if I persisted.

And so, January drags on into February. The cold, bleak days are still with us. They are getting longer, we're told, but it doesn't feel like it. From my bedroom window I see snow on the mountain tops and I shiver in the morning cold. It's dark as I get up, just past 5 a.m., and all is quiet in the rest of the sleeping house. I eat some porridge to warm me up before I head out onto the icy roads to drive to Thurles and catch the morning train to Dublin. It's a four-hour round trip I make two or three times a week but this is the sacrifice I made to be living in the countryside. My work might be in Dublin but my heart and soul are in rural Ireland, far from the bustling capital.

This day ahead will be like any other with its ups and downs, but I have one thing to help me get through it. I smile to myself and know I'll be able to let the stresses subside. For tomorrow is the end of the week and I will be out on the river again. It's been weeks since my journey to the Drowes on New Year's Day and I haven't been fishing since.

January has come and gone as quickly as the setting sun of winter. The opening of Lough Currane on the fifteenth I missed; the early-season promise of Carrowmore Lake went unfulfilled, while talk of a day fishing for pike was left idle. Before I knew it, January was at an end.

But tomorrow is 1 February and the opening of the season on the River Blackwater in Cork, only a thirty-minute drive from home. I'll be back out on the river wading through its waters on the hunt for salmon again. Just me, the river, a fish if I'm lucky, and all that nature has to offer for those precious few hours.

In Irish it is 'An Abhann Mhór', the Big River, rising in the Mullaghareirk mountains in Kerry, flowing south and east into Cork, passing through Mallow and Fermoy, then entering Waterford at Lismore and flowing out to the sea at Youghal. It is a river famed for its salmon from years gone by, and while the catches, like everywhere else, have plummeted, it is still one of Ireland's main salmon rivers. Its wide stretches, long, smooth glides and enticing, deep pools are the perfect features for salmon to make their runs upstream to spawn.

The Blackwater is always foremost in my mind at this time of year and it is a river that holds a special place for me. It's where I first learned to fly fish for salmon, and to throw a line across the water in search of that elusive fish. Since then, the grace and artistry of Spey casting is something I've come to appreciate even more, an aesthetic guile to aim for while I'm not catching fish.

The casting of a double-handed rod, culminating in the D-loop and shooting of line to the far riverbank, is a sight to behold. Glenda Powell, the woman who taught me to Spey cast on the Blackwater, is a master of the art. A fly rod in her hands is like a paint brush in the hands of an accomplished artist. With small, gentle strokes of the rod tip, Glenda coaxes the fly line to where she wants it to go – out over the water in an effortless display of loops and arcs.

Demonstrating with the deftest of touches, she lifts the line out of the water, casting it behind her and, in one fluid forward-momentum movement, flicks the rod tip forward, effortlessly casting out 80 yards of line onto the river before us. As the last few yards uncoil themselves and almost give themselves up before her touch, you can only watch in amazement at the timing and skill required to be able to perfect such technique. From her 'office' on the riverbank, Glenda takes me through the chinks in my casting technique. Watching you, she can spot a fix that will set you on your way and leave you with a confidence and belief in yourself that yes, you are now a fly angler.

I have come to love the Blackwater and Glenda's beats, almost as if they are home waters. While the Suir is less than ten minutes away and a regular haunt, especially for trout during the summer evenings when I have an hour or two to spare, the Blackwater is the river I find myself being drawn to with the hope of a salmon on my line.

Glenda Powell says fishing has given her her life, her family, her kids. 'True happiness is when it doesn't matter what day of the week it is,' she says with a smile. Aside from being an Irish fly casting world champion (how few and far between are they?) she was also the first woman to achieve both the salmon and trout Association of Professional Game Angling Instructors certificates for teaching.

Her journey has been a long one, but it never wavered from its path. 'My uncle Mike died when I was nine,' she explains. 'He was a keen fisherman, and he must have noticed my interest in fishing because he left me his rods and flies.'

With her uncle's rod in her hands, she stood on the bank of the local River Inler, a small river which flows through Comber in County Down where she lived. Unable to cast out the line properly, however, she learned to stick with it. It was a lesson that stood to her in the struggles she endured over the next few years and which would help shape and determine her future life. But she was, literally, hooked.

'It's just something I loved to do and had to do. I would get up first thing in the morning before school and go down to the river to fish. After school I would come home, change out of my uniform and head back to the river, fishing until it was late. I just loved it so much.

'I took so long to learn how to cast properly – I was fifteen

before I felt competent and confident. I was receiving advice of course from older fishermen on the riverbank – much of it bad advice though, mind you! But I was very determined. I knew that this was what I wanted to learn; I knew that if I persevered I could do it. Finally, after about four or five years I was getting there, but I also knew I still had a long way to go.'

While her father loved shooting and her family life growing up was an outdoors one – 'We would have ducks, geese, ferrets around the place' – she was the one who pursued fishing with a passion and obsession that she knew wasn't going to go away.

At eighteen, when college or working life beckoned, Glenda made the decision to try to eke out a living working at her passion, travelling to Scotland hoping to somehow fish and find work in fishing.

Ask any would-be writer, actor or artist, and they will tell you how hard it is to put food on the table and pay the bills doing something you really enjoy. So hard, in fact, that for most people it is an ideal that they have simply given up on.

'I drove from Northern Ireland to Scotland,' Glenda says of her eighteen-year-old self. 'I had £1,000 in my pocket and because I was told there were jobs in Aberdeen, I drove there and realised this was actually a really big city! I left it quickly and came across, quite by accident, the famous and beautiful River Dee. All I could think of was: how can I get to fish on that river?

'I found a house I could rent a few miles down the road and soon I was working in a nearby nursing home so I could earn enough to be living and fishing. I still couldn't afford to fish on the Dee though.'

It was while she was working in the nursing home that Glenda met a woman called Mrs Chidsey, a resident in the home who would have a lasting impact on her life. 'She looked at me one day and asked me what was I doing working there. I told her to pay for a living. But then she asked me what was it I really wanted, and I told her: to be fishing. Every day then Mrs Chidsey would keep at me, asking, "What are you doing today to make your dream happen?"

'Soon afterwards, inspired by Mrs Chidsey, I entered a competition to be on the Scottish Ladies international fly fishing team and I came second and qualified to be on the team – the youngest to qualify. I was starting to get somewhere now and through competitions I was becoming known. I then applied for and got my instructing qualifications in trout and salmon fishing from the Scottish Anglers National Association, and it looked as if things were starting to come together for me in Scotland.'

However, her father took ill and she returned to Northern Ireland, leaving Scotland behind her just as it seemed things had finally been on an upward curve.

'I was back to square one,' she says. 'I started working in nursing homes again as a care assistant to earn a living. But my father got better and I started branching out and getting involved in different areas of fishing. I set up my own fly fishing instructing company, became a rep for a tackle company, was managing the Irish Ladies fly fishing teams, and was writing some fishing articles.

'I was doing about five different things, but you had to, you see. You had to juggle loads of balls at once to put it all together to earn enough. But I was loving it. I was getting to travel around the country, I was fishing, and I was involved in fishing. That was all that mattered to me.'

It was while writing an article for a fishing magazine that she ended up on the Blackwater, and she fell in love with the river and its valley right away. Twenty years later she's still teaching and guiding on the river for eight months of the year. It's her home, her spiritual place of being.

She has finally arrived at a place where she eats, sleeps and breathes fishing every day. 'It has come full circle for me,' she admits. 'I'm not fighting for it to happen anymore. I am doing what I want to do. I have lived a full life.'

For Glenda, the real pleasure is in teaching, not competing, and seeing more women and children getting involved in fly fishing. Recently she was asked to put down her thoughts on paper as to why she fishes, and for days she struggled to pinpoint just what it is that drives someone to pursue one thing over all others, no matter what.

From that day as a nine-year-old when she was handed her uncle's rods, to becoming a world champion at just thirty-one, how could she explain that inner passion, that feeling we all wish we could nurture and cherish?

'It is the hope, the wonder, the childlike excitement and the never-ending learning that drives me,' she finally wrote. 'It is the Peter Pan syndrome, the waders, the puddles, the sausages on the camp fire, the kettle brewing and the fishing in the rain. It is the flowing river: like life itself, it keeps on moving over obstacles, turning and twisting on its way to the sea.'

While trout fishing has its allure with attention to fly life and matching the hatch, salmon fishing has none of these intricacies or niceties. Cast a line out, have a fly imitate something, anything, whatever the hell will work, and try to entice the salmon to eat when it doesn't want to – what's not to like about the impossible challenge being presented? But I like the process of flailing, practising, flailing some more, and finally getting that sweet-spot feeling that it's all starting to come together. Of course it usually happens in the last week of the season in September just before the closed season of three months begins and you can't fish anymore.

How is it, I wonder, that whenever I book a lesson with Glenda and am in the water learning to cast, conditions are perfect? There's no sign of a breeze, the water is just above my knees, gently lapping my waders while I stand on a flat, gravel surface in a smooth flow. Isn't this what it's supposed to be like all the time?

Until, that is, the first time you go out on your own, you wade into a beat where the water is a foot above where it should be and conditions feel more like you're in the Atlantic facing down incoming waves than in an inland river flowing through a pastoral landscape.

As for the forward cast and shooting a line out, you look as if you're trying to slap yourself in the face with a stick and you fail so miserably that your line ends up 10 feet in front of you. Yes, it can feel that bad.

So many permutations, so many things that can go wrong. Twisting and turning, keeping on moving, it's our daily struggle in life and on the water. But this is what makes it all the more beautiful and enriching when it *does* come right. Just when you think you've nailed it, something else gets thrown in your way. And that of course is just the casting part. We haven't even got to the fishing for salmon, a fish whose numbers have been decimated. What can you do but just go fishing and not think too much about it all? Anything else is a bonus.

And so, on 1 February this year, I find myself heading south on the M8 once more. I have come to meet fellow anglers, walk the river and observe the ritual and the ceremony of the opening day of the season on the Blackwater River. Glenda's beat is at Upper Kilmurry: it's the part of the river where she gives her lessons in front of the fishing hut that has heard a thousand fishing tales, not all of them true. We're in the Blackwater Valley where the river cuts through the land between Fermoy and Lismore. Behind are the Knockmealdowns with Tipperary on the other side but on this side sweeping in wide bends through fields of dairy cows is the Blackwater.

In the morning, with a heron watching from the far bank, as part of her traditional ceremony Glenda reads poems and salutes the life-flowing river by pouring whiskey into the waters, marking the start of another season on the Blackwater.

Like the rituals and observations of the Church, we anglers follow our own traditions, paying homage to the seasons, nature and the rivers. Christianity has Saint Brigid's Day for rebirth and renewal; fly anglers have the opening of the Blackwater, and in much the same way the fly fishing season follows nature's old, well-worn path. It gives me a sense of comfort, of structure, marking out the year in this way. Everything has a beginning and this is why I am here.

Along with the half dozen other anglers I walk back to the fishing hut where a warm stove is blazing to keep out the icy February air. Around the room sit Glenda, her partner Noel and an assortment of regulars to these parts. Some have whiskey glasses in their hands, others warm cups of tea, all sitting back enjoying the comforts of the room surrounded by pictures of anglers and salmon from days gone by.

After a few minutes I venture outside to walk down to the river and get a feel once more for her ebbs and flows. The water rushes by fast and heavy at this time of the year, its colour peaty after the heavy January storms just gone. Unfortunately the river is too high to be fishing and I will have to wait another week at least before it drops to a more manageable height.

Instead, I spot a few snowdrops nestled in the grass as I walk downstream, the first signs of early spring and promise of hope. I'm grateful to be back walking familiar ground, grateful for the promise of the year to come and for more days like this away from the humdrum and noise of the working week. It also feels like I'm slowly getting to know the Blackwater better, slowing myself down to the river's pace – well, at least this stretch of it – and I've made friends along the way as well.

'What more could you want?' Glenda often says to me as we sit outside the hut gazing out at the river, chatting about life's ups and downs, deaths, illnesses and struggles.

'It's the same for all of us, whether you're a high-powered financier in the city or running a fishing lodge in the countryside,'

I remind her, and she acknowledges and agrees, though not all of our paths end up the same.

We grow up as kids dreaming of being our own heroes and stars. Then somewhere along the way we lose sight of who we are and before we know it, we're in a job that we know won't keep us happy forever. Life catches up on you, there's a mortgage to pay, kids to feed and soon you're thirty, forty, fifty …

Maybe it truly is the life of quiet desperation, as penned by Thoreau. Some say the answer is as simple as looking back to when we were children and rediscovering what it was that lit up our worlds and hearts. Was it writing stories, building things, or drawing pictures? Witness the night classes full throughout the year and see how many people want to rediscover 'something' that they know lies within them, something that will give them the 'beginner's mind' openness of childhood. It might not be the panacea and the key to happiness, but at least it gives them hope and belief, something beyond the daily grind.

The only faith that matters is in what you are doing every day. In belief and happiness that what you are doing is truly part of who you are and what you are here to do. However, most of us gave up that dream somewhere between our teens and twenties and lost our way. It is to the bravest, the most determined, to the few like Glenda Powell, those who would not give up, that we must salute. They are the 10 per cent. The survivors. The rest of us are lost in our jungles struggling each day to get out.

Just being able to walk here as I reach the bend at the Lug Pool and take a seat on one of the bankside benches looking downstream to where the river continues on – that is contentment enough for me. For now, for today, at least.

But there's a river down the road from me and tomorrow I will fish. I will get to be free and dream once again – if only for a few hours.

3.

*At Home
on the Suir*

March is a strange month. Bitterly cold, icy winds driving through the garden and fields, woolly hats still needed. Yet the daffodils are emerging, and some days the sun is shining with a warmth that reminds you spring is in the air.

Saint Patrick's Day is the main highlight of course, mainly because of the bank holiday and the day off work that it brings. We stand in the town for the parade, watching the tractors and trucks drive by while the kids have their hats at the ready to catch any sweets that might come raining down from the 'floats'. It's not quite on a level with Macnas-spectacle theatrics, but the Irish flags are flying and it's a day to be proud to be Irish.

My own memories as a kid are pretty much the same. I grew up in Raheny in the north Dublin suburbs and every 17 March would be brought in to the city on the bus with my sister to stand on Dame Street in the freezing cold for what seemed like hours as one float after another drove slowly by. The highlight was the American brass bands, so loud and colourful blasting their way through the parade in perfect formation, announcing themselves to one and all like only Americans can.

Half the people in the crowd seemed to be American as well, flying over in their thousands to come back to the 'auld sod' for their celebration of Irishness in leprechaun jumpers and hats. We all thought them rather odd, but their sheer delight at being in Ireland was childlike and innocent. Saint Patrick's Day was a time for kids and visitors.

And yet I'm an outsider too as I stand with the boys outside the Aldi supermarket for the much smaller, local version of the Saint Patrick's Day parade in south Tipperary over thirty years later. You won't hear many Dublin accents down this part of the country and come All-Ireland time it's hard to get as excited as the locals when Tipperary's hurlers are on the hunt for the Liam MacCarthy cup. My boys have both Tipp and Dublin jerseys and I'll always get them to cheer on the Dubs in football and Tipp for the hurling. With parents from both places, they can have the best of both worlds, I tell them.

As we watch the tractors and trailers chug on by, there's a potpourri of accents all around us. It's not the American twang from parades when I was a child that I hear now, but the sounds and voices of Poles, Latvians, Brazilians and Asians who have come out to celebrate our patron saint's day.

When the boys have caught their fill of sweets in their leprechaun hats and when they start to complain of the cold in their bones we move on, leaving the last remnants of the parade behind.

'Can we go to the playground for a while?' they ask me, and I say okay. 'Just keep running around, that will warm you up,' I tell them.

There's only one other boy in the playground when we get there, watched over by his grandfather. 'Fifteen minutes,' I tell them as they run off, feeling my own legs start to freeze up.

Normally you'd keep to yourself in the playground, follow

your kids around as they play and shout, running from the bridge to the castle to the slide, the swing, the roundabout, see-saw and back again, lost in the world of their making.

Occasionally, if your child is playing with another kid, you'd chit-chat to the parent.

'What age?'

'Isn't he tall?'

'What's his name?'

'He's a great climber.'

And on it would go for a few more minutes before you both retreat into silence, smiling, watching your kids go screaming around the castle once more.

When it's busier, the voices and shouts of five-, six-, seven-, eight-year-olds fill the air, a cacophony of high-pitched happiness jumping, tumbling, running, falling. Today, though, it was quieter, just my boys and the one other kid, with the freedom of having the place to themselves.

The other boy was a confident lad, running straight over to where my boys were playing and introducing himself to them. At the same time, his grandfather came over and stood right beside me.

'What age are your boys?'

There was a smoker's wheeze to his voice.

'Six and four,' I replied. 'And yours?'

'Jake – my grandson – he's five. You're Irish?'

'A Dub, ye,' I said. Dub first, Irish second, was my stock reply. I may have been living in Tipperary for over a decade, but I was still a Dub. An outsider beyond the Pale, which was how

I liked it. But I had a feeling now where this was going. These conversations always started out this way.

'A Dub? Well, at least you're Irish. I'm not racist but sometimes it seems like they're in the majority, you know?'

This could go one of two ways and I wasn't going to spend any longer listening to an old man's rant. I followed my boys as they raced across to the swings.

'Okay, boys, time to head home, let's go eat your sweets.'

Reluctantly they jumped down from the swings, but they were also eager to start opening their goodies. We returned home, stiff from the cold, but the kids were on a sugar high and delighted with themselves.

I left them to their sweeties and grabbed my rod and bag. 17 March is also the opening of the season on my local River Suir in south Tipperary and I needed to be out in the air. The brief conversation in the playground left a sour taste and I didn't want it as a reminder of the day. With the kids occupied at home, now was a good chance to slip away.

I turned off the local road down to the Ballybrado beat. For two minutes I drove slowly down the overgrown track; there's always a last bend to come around before I arrive at the river and once around this, my line of sight is clear and I will know immediately if there are other anglers that have got there before me.

Today I am the only one there as I park beside the river. It's in full flow at this time of year with a tinge of brown to it from rain showers the day before. I walk to the edge and take it all in. Back to the Suir for another season, back to the familiar beat. Upstream is the flat, slow-moving river, perfect for a dry fly on a summer's evening, while downstream are deep pots and holes with trees and bushes hampering any easy casting. In front of me the water is riffled and fast, knee to waist height, perfect for wading and casting a nymph into. In the distance an old ruin looks down from a hill and I can hear lambs bleating for their mother in the field nearby.

It's been a long six months since I was last here. It's longer in fact, as I think back and try to work out the last time I stood on this spot. It must have been maybe nine, ten months ago. But here I am on the first day of the season, resolved to get here more often and make the most of having this wonderful river and its fishing only minutes from my door.

This early in the season, most times you have the beat to yourself. I've met tourist anglers – French or English mainly – who might be over for a few days. They're usually nymphing, and doing a good job of it too. When I get talking to them by the riverbank they always marvel at what an incredible river the Suir is, how lucky I am to have it near to home.

'And it's usually so quiet,' they say.

'I'm not from around here either,' I admit to them. But you're right, it is an untapped jewel.'

The only time I've found the Ballybrado beat busy is in the evening during a summer's rise but I've also fished it in perfect conditions with fish rising all around me without another soul around. It's part of the allure, the visiting anglers tell me: 'Fishing in Ireland is so untouched.'

Only a handful of locals I know of show much interest in fishing or the river and sometimes it takes an outsider to show them what they've got. My wife is astonished at how I know so many back lanes and fields to get to the Suir and I've brought the family to scenic places nearby that she says she never even knew existed.

'It takes a Dub to show you culchies,' I laugh.

'You can't use the word culchie!' she tells me, shaking her head.

'I'm a Dulchie,' I say in protest. 'I've always liked being an outsider.' Growing up in suburban Dublin it was the countryside I hankered after; and while I should have been supporting Leinster in the rugby, it was always Munster I was cheering for – even before I had met my future wife and moved to Tipp.

From childhood I've felt an affinity to the countryside that I never felt around housing estates and the busyness of city life. But now that I'm actually living in rural Ireland, I make sure to hold onto my Dublin background, still going to Croke Park on match days to see the Hill in full flow when the Dubs are in action on the pitch. I also relish leaving it all behind me – no more traffic lights every fifty metres, no more dealing with rude and irritable shopkeepers, no more rush and noise, buildings and people crowding in on me. My spirit feels lifted as I drive onto the M7 and know I'm heading south for Tipperary. On the motorway a BMW cuts in front of a car, which flashes its lights in anger. Cars, bumper to bumper, are hooting and giving out as the BMW speeds away across other lanes. A city of angry people going where? Thankfully, soon the busy traffic filters away off to the other exits to Kildare, Carlow, Portlaoise and after ninety minutes, when I see the peaks of the Galtees in the distance, I know I'm not far and it begins to feel like home.

Maybe it feels like home because I've embraced what's around me in the area, from the fishing to the GAA; trying to make the most of what's on offer and getting to know the locals in the process. It was the same when I emigrated to Sydney with my family when I was ten. It was daunting and terrifying leaving Ireland behind for a new life on the other side of the world, but I threw myself into everything that school and sport had to offer.

My circle of friends that I made there were Tamer of Egyptian descent, Lisa from a South American family, Alex of Italian stock and Fernando who didn't seem quite so sure where he came from. We were kids from a melting pot of countries from around the world and I was accepted almost immediately, especially as I was decent at soccer in the playground.

Now my own boys have friends with names such as Samir and Kasper, as well as Aidan and Cormac. Ireland has found the world and the world has found Ireland, even in a small village in south Tipp.

As I began to fish the Suir more and more, I was slowly beginning to realise how important a river it has been and appreciated by locals and visitors alike.

The Suir's reputation has long been known to anglers – for salmon and brown trout – but it's for the dry fly fishing that it is perhaps most famous, full of hard-to-catch wily trout.

Lord Edward Grey of Fallodon, the British foreign secretary from 1905 to 1916, who uttered the famous words, 'the lights are going out' at the beginning of the First World War, was a passionate fly angler and described the Suir as the most challenging river he came across.

'The first time I saw this river was late in August,' he wrote in his 1899 book *Fly Fishing*. 'The water ran in all sorts of channels between beds of bright green weeds ... One could wander for miles all day about the most extraordinary variety of water but there were trout enough for dry fly fishing. Half-a-dozen or so might be found rising near together ...

'I was warned that at this season of the year, when the water was low, I must not expect to catch any of these fish, but I cared nothing for warnings. The trout were there and were rising ... These trout, however, at first upset my calculations. They brought me face to face with a difficulty which did not exist on the ticket water at Winchester – they were unapproachable. Never was an angler more put upon his mettle ... For two days they defeated me utterly ... It was the wildest and most exciting and most fascinating dry fly fishing that I have ever had ...'

It all sounds familiar over a hundred years on, as does his description of his desire to escape work to go fishing come the weekend: 'If our work will let us escape on Friday evening, it is luxury,' he wrote. 'But even if we belong only to those in the middle state of happiness, who work till midnight or later on Friday, and can have the whole of Saturday and Sunday in the country, we may still be splendidly well off, provided that we are careful to miss nothing.'

Working till midnight and only getting away from it all on a Saturday and Sunday – and they say modern work and society has us at breaking point.

But fly fishing in the nineteenth century and for a lot of the twentieth century as well was a divided, class-riven sport. As

Shane Gallagher from the Drowes recounted, his family couldn't legally fish the river for hundreds of years despite living next to it. Fishing and the fish within a river were the domain of the gentry who owned the land next to it, and in Irish historical terms that invariably meant the Protestants, many of whom were absentee landlords living in England, and it was the local Catholics who were to be kept from it.

Water bailiffs were a common sight on the Suir and illegal fishing resulted in cases before the courts. The fee of 10 shillings for a single salmon licence and £1 for a cross line and a rod licence in the 1800s was also a barrier to entry for the lower classes to the sport.

To help drive anglers (the right type, of course) to the river, successful and large catches of fish were proudly proclaimed to the local press for publication. One reads of Colonel Browne of the 93rd Highlanders killing two salmon each weighing 33 lbs, while in 1874 the rod-caught Irish record salmon of 58 lbs was taken on the river near Ardmayle, between Holycross and Golden, by Michael Maher.

Each time I visit my local Ballybrado beat, as I walk upstream I cross a metal footbridge where stands a sign commemorating William Joshua Ffennell. Ffennell was born in 1799 into a family of sixteen at Ballybrado, the big house overlooking this stretch of the river, and growing up, he cared more for country sports than formal education.

In many ways, he was an early precursor of today's environmental campaigners but he was also a champion of fishery owners and their rights in keeping the ordinary people away from what was an illegal food source for them.

It was the years leading up to the Famine, and violence and lawlessness was increasing between locals and the 'outsiders', those of the ruling class who held the keys to power and to provision.

A speech by Ffennell's friend the earl of Glengall in the House of Lords in 1837 gave an insight into just how violent the situation on the rivers had become.

'Terrible Conflict. An immense concourse of persons went down the river in cots on Tuesday, for the purpose of destroying the weirs between this city and Duncannon, which have been illegally erected, and are destructive, in a great measure, to the salmon of the Suir. They proceeded vigorously in their work of levelling until they had been seen by the county of Wexford people, who assembled in great numbers to the banks, and succeeded in restraining them from further devastation.'

It is interesting to note how violent the clashes were, even leading to deaths, and it shows just how potent and emotive an issue it was with the Irish people; one can picture the Irish farmers and small landholders living near rivers like the Suir, which were teeming with fish, and not being able to get near them unless by illegal means. Ten years after Glengall's speech, the worst year of the Famine struck, with the death of more than a million people from starvation.

Even with Irish independence after 1921, many of the fishing rights remained in private hands – and still do – but clubs like the Cahir and District Anglers Association on the Suir, that I'm a member of, have opened up access for many.

William Ffennell's life is a reminder of the long and tortuous relationship – when it came to fishing rights – between the landowners and the people but ultimately, for him, it was about conservation and preservation and in 1863 a salmon act for Ireland was passed, which finally got rid of the stake weirs after nearly thirty years of campaigning. A similar act was then passed for England in 1865 and just two years later Ffennell died in London, on 12 March 1867, his life's work having come to fruition.

But now, in the twenty-first century, the plight of the salmon is an even more pressing one. Gone are the days of hauls of salmon from the Suir. Few salmon are seen this far upstream and any that are caught are usually on waters thirty miles below near Carrick-on-Suir.

As a result, much of the focus of rivers is moving away from fishing to other outdoor pursuits such as walking, swimming and kayaking, with stretches of the Suir from Cahir down to Carrick now designated as a Blueway to try and entice more people to the area to use the river in another way.

But at least the brown trout have survived and are still there and the river is not to be under-estimated. 'It [the Suir] has everything, incredible numbers of fish, and a choice of all the different type of fishing you want,' Mike Drinan, an Irish international fly angler who has fished competitively all over the world, told me once. 'Plus it's not easy, it's a challenging river, but it's right up there with anywhere in the world.'

The Suir has a reputation as a river with fish not easily fooled and it is a reputation well-deserved. I've spent hours on sessions failing to land a rising fish, throwing my hands up in frustration, questioning my sanity and whether I'd have been better off taking up golf. The joy of course is in those moments when it does fall right and it does come together. Then all is right with the world again.

For the numerous frustrating sessions, the one that hits the mark is usually nothing less than memorable. That's the thing about Suir trout, when you do crack them (if only for an evening), a world of jewelled brownies awaits.

It's far from perfect today on Saint Patrick's Day as I set off upstream crossing the small metal bridge, passing the Ffennell memorial and walking alongside the river's banks. There's no other angler on this stretch today and I don't blame them. An icy wind blows downriver and the water is flowing fast. If I was a fish on this kind of day, I wouldn't be inclined to be caught, I think to myself as I scan across to the far bank.

But still, I'll stay out for an hour so, casting the line and watching my wet flies slip downstream with the current trying to fool a hungry trout, celebrating Saint Patrick's Day in my own way. I'm walking the same steps that William Ffennell took two hundred years earlier, except this time I'm permitted to fish for the salmon and trout. Some battles are won and lost, but some are worth fighting on for.

I watch my line as it goes down and across, the only sound the ripples of the flow and the sudden beating of the wings of a heron that I've intruded upon. He flies up, annoyed, but settles again further downstream.

There is something mysterious and alluring about the Suir. It stretches for miles through the land, ruined castles at once-important locations like Ardfinnan, Newcastle and Cahir hinting at its past importance for trade, food and travel. It passes through a land of rich limestone fields of cows and crops of wheat and barley, and it's this same limestone that has made the river so abundant in fly life and trout.

Maybe it's because it's my 'local' river that I have such an affection for it; maybe it's the miles and miles of fishing available through the club; or maybe it's because of its place in the history and writings of fly fishing. But I find it a place that I can never truly understand. Stretches of the river like Ballybrado have become my church now, somewhere I go to get away from it all, a meditation of sorts, surrounded by nature. Morning or evening, I know I can take a trip to these peaceful surroundings, cast a line and feel like I'm back in the moment, rejuvenated once again by what life has to offer. Even as a Dub and an outsider, I feel I can finally call it home.

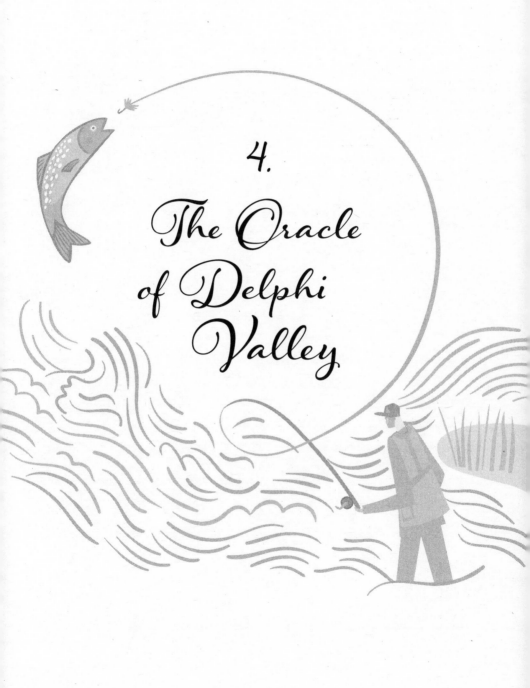

4.

The Oracle
of Delphi
Valley

*T*he Delphi Valley is majestic; the Delphi Valley is haunting; the Delphi Valley is striking; and the Delphi Valley is breathtaking. Towering over it in central Greece stands Mount Parnassus, while the Pleistos River flows through the land west until the Corinthian Gulf.

The land here is sparse, wild and steeped in history, renowned as the site where the Oracle resided, pronouncing on important decisions in the classical world and being the centre – or navel, even – of the world itself.

In mythology the links from Greece to Ancient Ireland run strong. According to the *Book of Invasions* written in the eleventh century as a history of Ireland from pagan mythological times, Ireland was taken six times by six different groups of people. The first three, the Cessairians, Partholonians and Nemedians, were forced to abandon the island but it was the Fir Bolg (or 'men of bags'), descendants of the Nemeds, now enslaved in Greece, who returned to Ireland and divided it into five kingdoms or provinces.

Of the Fir Bolg, Gann took north Munster, Sengann took south Munster, Genann took Connacht, Rudraige took Ulster, while Slanga took Leinster. Tara became the seat of the high king, the one to rule over them all, with Slanga the first. But their reign wasn't to last long as soon after, the Tuatha Dé Danann, other descendants of the Nemed, arrived.

They were said to have landed at Connacht in dark clouds and were known as the 'tribe of the gods' due to their superior intelligence and knowledge of the sciences, art and magic. They defeated the Fir Bolg high king, Eochaid mac Eirc, at the Battle of Mag Tuired and subsequently ruled Ireland, exiling the Fir Bolg to Connacht. In Celtic mythology the Tuatha are the original gods of Ireland, the deities of the Celtic world representing the natural world, protecting humans from their destructive selves.

However, a sixth and final people, the Milesians, said to have come from Spain, invaded Ireland. Led by Amergin, the Tuatha conjured a great wind to stop the Milesians landing but instead Amergin's song calmed the wind and the Milesians came to Ireland, conquering and finally settling it. The Tuatha were said to have been driven underground where they were forced to dwell in the 'otherworld'. The Irish land is a history of settlers and invaders and even the word 'Gael' is an old Irish word for 'foreigner'.

Take a drive out west, past Clifden, towards Leenane and Killary Harbour, and you are in a land where time has taken a back seat. Leenane is a small, sleepy village at the head of a sixteen-kilometre fjord, Ireland's only fjord, nestled between the Maamtrasna and Maamturk mountains on either side. At the height of summer, tour coaches crowd the narrow roads and the Fir Bolg and Tuatha Dé Danann might echo in your thoughts as you take the road towards Louisburgh, the peaks of the Mweelrea mountains looming large, as the road cuts into the valley itself.

Haunted by Waters

This is the Delphi Valley, so-called because it is said to be similar to that land in Greece. The rocky, barren landscapes bear much in common, not least the enduring links to mythology and the past. But this part of the west of Ireland goes back farther than any Protestant landowner whose Greek ideals were superimposed on a Gaelic landscape. For this is the land also of the people of the Mac ind Óclaichs, the townland of Tamhnaigh Fhionnlocha, and the lakes of Doo Lough and Finlough, a land of ancient history of its own before the Delphi moniker was applied. It's a valley with a history of tragedy and ills, a darkness haunting in its own rugged beauty.

Nevertheless Delphi was the name that stuck and it remains unique amongst the Connemara heritage and land. Its exotic name lingers still because its most recent history has also been exotic and foreign.

It's April and I'm driving into the valley on one of those days when the sun shines in the west of Ireland and you think the whole world should flock here to witness its wonder. I'm past Clifden, past the shamrock shops with their leprechaun signs, and travelling further north into wilder parts to meet with Peter Mantle, a visitor to these shores who ended up staying and rearing a family in one of the wildest, most remote parts of the country. The Delphi Valley, the estate and the fishing lodge have developed their own rich history all thanks in no small part to Peter.

I have always been fascinated and bewitched by this part of Connemara, not least by the name, and seeing the pictures of the former hunting and fishing lodge nestled in the Delphi Valley where it seems as if time itself stands still. There is the abundance of rivers and streams flowing through this rugged landscape making their short journeys to the Atlantic carrying the salmon and sea trout out to the ocean; then there are the echoes of the past all around. I don't know if it's the craggy rocks standing so bare and visible, so often shrouded in clouds, or the unpeopled land, but it doesn't take a huge leap of imagination to be transported back to the legends of the Tuatha Dé Danann and the Milesians.

I drive into Leenane and follow the road around Killary Harbour. I drive over bridges and pass by stone cottages and have the Bundorragha River for company all the way up into the valley. The black gates to Delphi Lodge are open but I won't be driving in to fish there today. Later in the year, I promise myself, I will be back to catch salmon.

Instead, I drive on, leaving the lodge behind. The road veers steeply upwards now to where I see the turn-off for the house and pull in to meet Peter Mantle upstream of Delphi. It's a wonderfully evocative stone cottage that opens out onto the flowing waters he had built his life around. I'm here because Peter came to this area as an outsider from England nearly forty years before. He came with a dream of a salmon lodge and a salmon fishery and amidst the rugged land and poor economic conditions of Ireland in the 1980s saw only potential, blinded by his love of fishing. But today, Delphi is not his anymore, time and life moves on, I find out, as we sit down for a lunch of brown bread and salmon, so rich and tasty it's a meal in itself, and I listen to his story.

If it wasn't for a salmon fishing trip on the Blackwater, on the Ballyhooly beat upstream of Fermoy, the story of how

Delphi Lodge became famous the world over might never have happened at all, Peter explains.

'I was living in America, working in financial journalism at the time and I'd been on a fishing holiday with a pal from London. We met up in Ireland and went fishing down to the Blackwater. By lunchtime, we were in the pub and got chatting to the bar lady and she said, "Do you know the fishing is for sale?" I said, "What?" and she said, "You know it's only £90,000." That was £90,000 Irish pounds which at the time was about £70,000 sterling. My mate, Robin, his mom had just died, and he had inherited £60,000 sterling. He said, "Jesus we should buy it."'

You get a sense of Peter Mantle's loquacious style as soon as you start talking to him. He is open, gregarious company, someone you could imagine spending hours holding court around a dinner table – which is exactly what he ended up doing.

'All we could find out,' he continues, 'was that the guy who owned it was called Hirsch and he lived in Toronto. Eventually I got him, we met, and over lunch agreed to buy it all, consisting of a lovely Victorian house, the old castle and three miles of pretty good fishing on the Blackwater. For nothing, you know, really for nothing; the equivalent in Scotland would have been ten times the amount. But the bugger changed his mind and he pulled out, saying they had decided to keep it.

'By this stage though our blood was up and the idea of having a bit of fishing, of being able to go to Ireland, really appealed to us. I started looking around for other places and wrote to lots of different people. Then somebody called John

Hamilton sent me three sets of particulars, one of which was for Delphi.'

The course of Peter's life was set to change as he and his business partner flew back to Ireland and made the long drive from Dublin to Galway and into the heart of Connemara, entering the Delphi Valley on a magical summer's evening when all seemed right with the world. Even though the house was run down, the atmosphere of the valley was entrancing, with the mountains looking down on them benignly and an angler fishing the lough in front of them.

'We went to meet the marquess of Sligo, Jeremy Altamont, who was trying to sell it, in Westport House and he wanted I think around £350,000 to £400,000 for it. He had no interest in fishing and to him Delphi was a bit of a liability; one of his many, many land holdings. We had some very tricky negotiations with him which were quite bizarre because in the middle of it all when we were poles apart on price he suddenly said, "I think we need a break here." We were in the library of Westport House and he said, "I'll show you around."

'The place is actually filled with fantastic artwork, with a massive collection of James Arthur O'Connor early nineteenth-century paintings, including several of Delphi, but he wasn't interested in any of that. What he wanted to show us was the pink rabbit suit that he dressed up in to bring in tourists. Now this is in the early days of trying to generate tourism to Westport House and we thought he was barmy; we looked at each other and semi-winked and decided we'd go back in and play hardball and we did and he collapsed on price. We agreed £250,000 and he then wanted another £3,000 for all the boats, engines and sticks of furniture that were left and we could see it was a matter of principle to him so we paid an extra grand and got it.

'But having got it we were unbelievably naïve – it was more or less a whim, we hadn't really thought through how we were going to do it, how were we going to make it work? The lodge was in a terrible shape and it was only a gradual realisation that, you know, this was going to cost a huge amount of money to keep it going and we had to find some way of paying for it on an ongoing basis.'

A health scare and hard living had brought Peter to this point where he was preparing to leave America and embark on a radically different career, one without financial security and in a completely different country. 'Give it a year,' he told his wife Jane and then she could decide if swapping modern life in America for the rural wilds of Connemara was to her liking.

Peter may have got his dream of owning some salmon fishing in Ireland and at a knock-down price – selling his flat in London effectively bought him the lodge, and the lakes and river in the valley – but making it work now was to be another question. Resourcefulness, though, is one of Peter Mantle's strengths.

'It was still way beyond our personal means so we put together a gang of pals, cousins, relatives – anybody we knew who liked fishing – and effectively built a kind of mini-syndicate of shareholders, including one or two who didn't even fish, and quite an eclectic group we had. We had a British army general which I kept very quiet about; we had a Tory MP's family trust; we had all my fishing mates; my pal Robin, he was an architect, he had a building development firm in London called Egg Builders and he and his mate both came in; we had a couple of academics.

'We had a really diverse group of people and the expectation was that they – if they liked fishing – would be able to come and stay pretty much whenever they liked, but we needed to raise more money for them to have somewhere to stay and the first thing we decided to do was to restore the cottages opposite Delphi Lodge. We never really dreamt that we would be able to restore the lodge itself, so Robin set about doing a little scheme for the cottages and then I was still doing a bit of journalism.

'I was doing a piece on the evils of timeshare which at the time was the subject of really nasty, heavy, dodgy sales mostly for apartments in Spain, but while researching the story I'd been up in Scotland talking to some of the posh land agents about how timeshare was working on salmon rivers, and the more I thought about it, the more I thought, wow you know that could work at Delphi. So I went to see this guy at Savills property agents, and said, "We're struggling with what to do with it and trying to find a way of financing it, would you come over and have a look?" He said, "Well, Peter, Ireland? I don't think so. We're not really into sea trout fishing and I gather it's mostly lake fishing, we're not really into that at all." I said, "Well come and see it," so we paid him to come over and took him down to the pub and took him fishing, and he fell totally in love with Delphi Valley, so they agreed to put the Savills name to our plan which gave it a brand of respectability. Then we launched an incredibly inexpensive timeshare syndicate where you would buy in for thirty years and you paid on average I think it was about £8,000.

'You got your cottage and fishing for two rods every year and it sold like hot cakes. Nobody'd ever done anything like it in Ireland before and before we knew where we were, people were flocking to see it and really liked it. It's very hard to understand how anybody could *not* like it and we then had enough money to start thinking about restoring the lodge itself as well as all the fishing facilities, new boats, new cottages, new everything.'

If it all seemed too easy, he soon found out that obstacles are never far away. These weren't problems of the physical or construction type, but a lot more serious and deep-rooted. The sea trout and salmon runs, which the fishery was famous for, collapsed nearly overnight. Unknown to Mantle, when buying the property and waters, a salmon farm was being opened in nearby Killary Harbour. None of the knowledge that exists today about the disastrous consequences of salmon farming on sea-run trout and salmon was around in the 1980s but by 1989 when the runs of fish disappeared, it was obvious where the blame lay.

'Here we were, with a fishing lodge and no fish. Like a pub with no beer,' he says ruefully. He wasn't one to be put off by a challenge like that, however, and there were to be more besides. At the top of the valley was allegedly Europe's richest find of gold, and plans for an open-pit mine were being quickly laid by developers looking to exploit the so-called mineral wealth below ground. Luckily for Mantle and the investors in the lodge, the gold find turned out not to be what was expected and the issue went away. The larger and lingering question of what to do about the salmon was still there, however.

'The only thing we could think of was to try and enhance

the salmon run. We found a guy, Dr David Piggins, who had pioneered salmon ranching at Burrishoole outside Newport, County Mayo in the 1960s. He had phenomenal success with his programmes, which were scientifically orientated and not commercially driven. But he liked the idea of helping us. We somehow managed to borrow £100,000 from the bank, who fortunately didn't really understand our business, and we built a hatchery, and prayed.

'And nothing happened, no salmon came back the following year. One appeared in 1991 but then forty to fifty in 1992, which was beginning to be interesting. In 1993 there were thousands of salmon coming back and Killary Harbour was jam-packed with them. Everywhere you looked there were salmon leaping. But that summer there was a drought and they couldn't get into the river and the nets took the lot of them. Perhaps 5,500 of our salmon, just carried out in the nets. I was fit to slash my wrists. Two out of every three fish were ours and I knew that because we had tagged and fin-clipped the hatchery fish that we released. But the good news was the fish were coming back and the hatchery was producing these extraordinary numbers of fish. It was unreal.'

Near the end of the decade over a thousand salmon were caught by rods at the Delphi fishery, far exceeding their expectations. If they had reached 200 salmon, Peter Mantle says, they would have been happy. That was the survival plan. This was turning out to be a lot better than that. It was commonplace now for an angler to come up for coffee mid-morning and slap three salmon down on the table.

  *Haunted by Waters*

Being British, Peter was conscious of being the outsider, however (despite his mother being Irish, summers spent in Ireland and being raised a Catholic), especially with the deep-seated resentment and history in the area dating back to the Famine. One of the most tragic stories and a long-stored memory is how a group of 600 starving men, women and children from Louisburgh walked the fifteen miles over the mountain pass to Delphi Lodge looking for food. The landlord was in the house eating his lunch but ignored their pleas and sent them away empty-handed. Emaciated and weakened, most of them died on the walk back, their corpses found by the grassy verge back up the mountain. A grey stone cross commemorating 'the hungry poor who walked here in 1849' stands there now, a bleak reminder of the tragedy. Looking down on the valley, amidst the barren landscape and mountain peaks, you can see that it is a place at the mercy of the wind, rain, cold and snow. One can only imagine the torment of having to walk all this way experiencing starving hunger only to be turned away to return the way they came. The countryside, bereft of crops or cows, is a constant reminder of the bare land and bare stomachs that afflicted so many for so long, a haunting reflection, all these years later, of the suffering once borne on the land.

'I've always been a little bit worried,' Mantle says when discussing his Britishness and how it would be received in the area. 'When we first arrived we put ourselves about a lot, seeing everybody in the valley, trying to explain that we were young and stupid and all we wanted was to try and put things back to how the lodge used to be. We'd even been to see the parish priest, who mistook my Filofax for a breviary, which was a great start! But nonetheless, for all practical purposes I was a Brit and acutely aware of the need to tread carefully.'

As with any new venture, the early years were the most precarious and the fishery and the proprietors' future hung on a knife edge.

'At times, we did think we might lose it all because we thought the bank might pull the plug and there were moments between 1990 and 1992 when we teetered on the brink of insolvency. So we launched another syndicate scheme to raise a bit more dosh to improve the hatchery, extend the lodge, and restore another couple of cottages on the estate to try and make it into a viable business that could actually wash its face and stood some chance of giving us an income sufficient to educate the kids. I'm not terribly interested in money but when you've got kids and a mortgage and all that sort of stuff obviously you have to start thinking a little bit more responsibly.

'Everything I got went into here. I absolutely loved it – I can't tell you how much. Even during the problems I really think if we hadn't had those, we might have got bored and gone, in a funny kind of a way. Fishing attracts an extraordinary array of people and what I liked was the great mix of people. We'd always done one huge dining table at Delphi with up to thirty people around it and I liked the idea of mixing people up. You could, quite literally, have a local Irish ghillie and some toff from England arguing about the correct tying of the claret bumble. I liked the interplay and I liked the fact that there was a theme of fishing that linked everybody in the room.'

The eclectic mix at Delphi and the evening mealtimes became the stuff of legend and it soon had the name of being the pre-eminent salmon fishery in Ireland. Prince Charles was a visitor (though was more interested in painting his watercolours than using his fly rod) as was former Sinn Féin vice-president and IRA commander in Derry, Martin McGuinness (though he wasn't at Delphi at the same time as Charles, obviously, Peter hastens to add). And whether you were royalty or not, you were still guaranteed a warm welcome and a good chance of landing a salmon.

'I became less and less interested in capturing fish myself and more and more interested in seeing new people catch fish in new places and trying new things,' says Peter. 'I still love fishing but I have always thought salmon fishing is a pretty weird form of madness. Anybody who does it is almost by definition eccentric because we're fishing for a fish that isn't feeding, we have no idea why they take a fly, which the great majority of the time they don't, and yet still we do it in the remote hope that we might be there at the odd moment when they decide they *will* take a fly!'

Appropriately enough, Peter's own fly fishing apprenticeship took place in Ireland over a number of school summers when he was sent to Millstreet in County Cork to stay with an aunt and uncle. The local postman, Jimmy Cotter, took him fishing on the Blackwater as well as shooting in nearby fields and ditches and showed him the ropes, providing the foundations that were to last a lifetime.

'I just thought it was fantastic so I came back year after

year after year for ten or twelve years. Jimmy tried to teach me everything he knew though I was a lousy student, and to this day I'm a bad shot and a pretty crappy fisherman but I loved all aspects of it including the afters in the pub, so I got the bug really early. My brother, who was with me that first night and caught nothing, didn't, and he doesn't understand it at all.

'I was always quite proud to have that Irish streak in me, you see. We've been here in this sort of idyllic unspoiled bit of Europe, and these are clichés, but with some of the most delightful people around. The quality of life and the people that you meet in the rural west of Ireland has been absolutely huge. There's very little real poverty anymore though and prosperity does change things.

'When we first came here, Martin, our fishery manager, used to row in regattas against guys from the islands who could not speak English. People have forgotten it was only thirty years ago that there were lots of kids in the Aran Islands who could not speak English. I remember hitchhiking around Ireland when I was about seventeen and every single vehicle would stop and give you a lift. You wouldn't go hitchhiking around now at all, things have become much more sophisticated with all the good and bad that entails.'

By the end of the 1990s, Peter Mantle had given his all to Delphi Lodge and come through the many obstacles and problems that had arisen throughout his ownership and running of the fishery. He was, by 1999, in his own words, suffering from exhaustion and thinking about doing another Delphi somewhere else while moving on to a less hands-on role.

With one eye on getting out, he sold his remaining shares,

which left him in a minority position for the first time in relation to Delphi.

'It was the biggest mistake I've ever made because the first few board meetings after 1999 were a catastrophe. I was suddenly dealing with people I didn't know and who knew even less about me and who weren't necessarily at all in line with what I thought they were. I tried to unravel everything and they wouldn't have it – they wouldn't sell – so then I thought, right, I'll take legal advice. Am I able to carry on doing what I've been doing for the past six years? The legal advice was yes, I told them okay I'm going to carry on running the show, I will operate within all the parameters that we agreed to make sure I don't fritter away business or your money but I'm not going to spend my life arguing with you at lengthy board meetings. Things settled down and they kind of got used to me and I to them, but I always knew if there was going to be an economic downturn, Delphi was fragile and they might pounce.'

Sure enough the economic downturn did come, and it wasn't just any downturn, it was the worst recession the country – or the world – had seen since the Great Depression of the 1930s. Tourism to Ireland collapsed as the important US market dried up completely, leaving Delphi in a very precarious position financially. Arguments at board level became commonplace and relationships were breaking down. 'Bugger this,' Peter thought. 'This isn't what I signed up for or wanted from Delphi, I'm off.' And with that he turned his back on the lodge and fishery, sold up and was gone.

The valley in Connemara may not have had Peter Mantle's skills or personality anymore, but there was to be a life after

Ireland, a Delphi dream that was coming to fruition: Delphi in the Bahamas.

'I'd always had this idea that what we were doing at Delphi was translatable into other environments. I discovered bone fishing in the Bahamas in the early nineties when it wasn't at all well known in Europe and my plan at that stage was to have this sort of double Delphi – each feeding off the other.

'We built the thing from scratch in the middle of nowhere in a beautiful location with a gorgeous building, and very close to good bone fishing. Everything on paper looked fantastic but behind the scenes there's all the bureaucracy you've got to deal with, all the approvals and licences. Then Lehman Brothers went bust in 2008 and every single deal evaporated. People forget how ghastly that autumn and winter were and there we were stuck with a half-built lodge with most of the money in place but still not enough to finish the job. A friend of mine in Nassau said, "Peter, let me take you to see my bank." We had hoped to do this without any bank borrowing at all, but we needed a million bucks to finish it and so, walking into the Royal Bank of Canada I said, "Look I've got five million in my pocket and I need another million." I must have got the only commercial loan advanced in the western hemisphere in October 2008.'

It was typical of Mantle. Even the great recession hadn't deterred him or his plans, and with the bank loan secured, Delphi in the Bahamas was completed and since then has proven to be as successful as its Irish counterpart. The 'formula', or whatever it is that Peter Mantle has been able to bring to the table, has been bottled and translated across the Atlantic to the

Caribbean. However, just as his Bahamas adventure was about to take off, illness struck and he was back in England having treatment, project managing from afar and putting further Delphi expansion plans on ice.

He came through it all, of course – as well as some of the fiercest hurricanes in Bahamian history – but he is now back living in England in semi-retirement running a small guesthouse and chalkstream dry fly fishing on the River Test in the Hampshire village of Nether Wallop. This is the quintessence of English country fishing and couldn't be farther from the wilds and rugged beauty of Delphi in the west of Ireland.

Ending up on the River Test was always at the back of his mind, he admits. When he and his wife Jane left Ireland behind, Delphi Bahamas was only ever going to be a ten-year plan and a fly fishing project in England would be his final one.

Although Connemara is in the past, there have been trips back for fishing and soaking up the surroundings. Each time he drives past the lodge though there must be some pangs of regret. After all, he got married there, raised kids and his family in this place, poured his life's blood, toil and sweat into making it a success, not just from a commercial perspective, but from a lifestyle aspect also. He gave so much to Delphi and it gave so much to him as well.

'The fact that we ended up becoming probably one of the better salmon lodges was a necessity rather than a result of any personal passion,' he says. 'I do genuinely think that salmon fishing is bonkers and that most of the people who do it are bonkers and I would include myself in that.

'But whatever I do I tend to do to the absolute maximum of my ability, probably at the expense of other things. Our place in the Bahamas encapsulates all that I might have aspired to. I feel I was very, very lucky to have stumbled across Delphi when I did at thirty-three. I was young at the time and you didn't think of hardships or difficulties at that age.

'How lucky we were to end up owning this extraordinary place in the middle of nowhere. We could not believe that anywhere so beautiful could have been abandoned but now here I am, I have nothing whatsoever to do with the business and yet I still adore the valley. I know this is a corny cliché and a lot of people say this, but I felt that we were only tenants of something special that we would pass on to future generations.'

Standing outside Peter's summer home, I listen to the river flow through the heart of the Delphi Valley. Running over the rocks of the mountain, this is the main artery of the Delphi system, up which the salmon come to the spawning grounds above us. There's a few sheep on the hills, an occasional otter and sparse wildlife. There are no people and it's as unspoiled as it was centuries ago. I can sense the history buried in the rocks as I take it all in. The landscape is raw, unspoilt and unchanged. From the Celts to the Famine to the tourists, the land has seen it all go by. The people and their stories weave some of their strands into the terrain but as time moves on it is the mountains, the rivers and these rocks that remain untouched.

'I was always very struck,' says Peter as we finish our lunch, 'by the fact that Brian Keenan, the author of that wonderful book on his time as a hostage in Beirut, said that his favourite spot to come to was the dock up at Doolough, to sit there of an evening and try and commune with nature. There is something vaguely spiritual about this valley and its slightly chequered history. It's special, it's incredibly tranquil, yet filled with a sense of foreboding and also thank God full of fish.'

5.
For More
Than a Day
on Lough
Corrib

*H*as there ever been something so inconsequential as an insect celebrated in song, poem, literature and even mobile phone ads? But then again, the mayfly is no ordinary insect.

Ephemera danica. From the Greek *ephemeros*, meaning lasting a day. There's always been something romantic and ethereal about life for just one day. Hatching, mating and then dying off. But it's not just the lifecycle, it's also the grace and size of the mayfly as she flutters over water, her sail-like wings making her seem like a miniature sailing boat floating along the rough seas of life. If ever there was an insect to be imagined through the human mind, it was the mayfly.

I knew I was in fly fishing country. As soon as I passed through Claregalway, the fly rods on cars began to be seen; B&Bs, hotels and lodges had pictures of leaping fish over their doors; the clearly marked yellow reg plates of UK cars were in abundance. They were all here for one thing, and looking out the car window, from time to time I could glimpse the water. Dipping in and out of view, she was there alright and I could feel my nerves heighten.

Driving an hour north of Galway, I was heading for Corrib: Ireland's mighty Lough Corrib. All 27 miles and 365 islands that dominated this part of the west of Ireland. It was May and I was going to be fishing during the madness of the mayfly season. 'Duffers' Fortnight' it's derogatorily called: two weeks of supposed easy fishing, when the trout go mad for the mayfly and anything lying on the water will supposedly catch them. Anyone can catch trout at this time of year, they say, even duffers.

If the Delphi Valley was stark, barren and haunting, this trip in May was in complete contrast. The first blooms of the mayflower herald the start of summer and the real beginning to the trout season. This is when summer starts to stretch out her arms into the long evenings and early mornings, when she flowers the hedgerows, gardens and fields, the trees coming into foliage and the countryside coming alive with colour, sounds and scents of warming gladness. I too felt like I was coming out of a slumber. The cold, dark evenings were finally giving way to light and heat. I had finished up a couple of busy projects, sometimes having to work six and seven days a week but the work had been finished, completed on time, and now, like Mole in *The Wind in the Willows*, I was burrowing out of my hole and coming up for some air again.

For the trout fisherman this time of year is magical: the mayfly will soon begin to hatch, their oversized sail wings, translucent in the light, a wholesome meal for hungry trout, eager to snatch without caution at easy pickings on top of the water, gorging themselves with wild abandon.

When word gets out that the 'mayfly are up', then the waiting fly anglers hit the road, bags and rods already packed and ready to go with no time to lose.

I envied those fly anglers who could depart at a moment's notice, many of them getting the boat from England, or those lucky few who could even follow the path of the mayfly hatching the more northerly one went, starting with Lough Derg; moving on to Corrib, Mask, Sheelin. These anglers would spend a few days on each water, taking advantage of the trout's new-found confidence, before moving onto the next lake to welcome the mayfly's arrival.

What a life, I thought. To be able to hit the road for weeks at a time, following in nature's path, fly fishing as you went along, capturing the best of what the brown trout fishing had to offer. I imagined driving around in an Amarok, packed to the brim with all the fly gear you could need or want, rods tacked to the bonnet and 'Living the fly fishing dream' emblazoned across the side of the truck with a fly rod in motion pictured underneath. I had seen such a truck once before, on the shore of Lough Currane outside Waterville in south Kerry – driven by not quite a trout bum, but probably the next best thing.

How many of us would love to live such a life, carefree and not tied down, able to drift along wherever your passion took you? If not fly fishing, maybe as a writer, painter, sculptor … to be your own boss, on your own time in this world. It's a common yearning of course, from the Epicureans up to Thoreau and the Beat generation, of people wanting to be free to come and go, to live in their own time. And while I may not be able to live beside Walden Pond as Thoreau once did, the next best thing are these days away, where, even if just for a day, I live out the imagined life.

And then Thoreau's words came drifting back, a refrain I had long ago tacked to my bedroom wall as a teenager but had lost along the way:

I went to the woods because I wished to live deliberately,
to front only the essential facts of life,
and see if I could not learn what it had to teach,
and not, when I came to die, discover that I had not lived.

This was to be my first time fishing the mayfly season and I had one day to experience what I could. I was coming into the Irish mecca of fly fishing and mayfly season was at its zenith. What could possibly spoil the next twenty-four hours?

But then, as I drove on, I had to push the wipers on the car to their top speed. What had started as a shower when I left Tipperary two hours ago had turned into a downpour. Not only that, but the wind was whipping the rain this way and that. The sky was a dark, foreboding grey. This was May and there wasn't a hint of blue sky anywhere. Luckily the rain jacket was in the boot, and the woolly hat as well, for the temperature was struggling to get into double figures.

I had been warned that the fishing had been getting more difficult in recent years, with fish harder to come by, and that any thoughts of 'Duffers' Fortnight' were wide of the mark. As I peered through the windscreen, the white horses visible on the water were a warning that even getting out onto the lake might be a struggle. I only had today – just this day away from the kids and family, a day to myself – and I was determined to make the most of it.

Luckily the rain clouds did subside just as I turned off the Tuam road and headed west for Corrib. The lake's northern end, around the sleepy village of Cornamona, was where I was headed.

I passed through the small village of Cong where the stately Ashford Castle is situated on the outskirts. Once the former home of the Guinness family, it is now a luxury five-star hotel. Range Rovers, BMWs and Audis were commonplace around the streets, while coffee shops tried to entice people in with promises of Irish soda bread, cakes and tea for that 'authentic' Irish experience. But what I was travelling towards was worth more than any soda bread in the world.

Winding through the narrow streets, you could feel time passing away. This was a thriving tourism spot where fly fishing was a lucrative side-trade for local businesses. The river flowing through added to the fishy air of the place, but I wouldn't be stopping. This wouldn't be the fly fishing I was practising. I was happy to leave the five-star luxury and manicured lawns behind as I headed onwards. I'd prefer the rugged locals cursing at the weather and the fishing gods telling me what life was really like trying to make a living on the edge of Corrib.

Through Cong and the road forked: one road to Clonbur, the main town in this part of the Galway–Mayo border lying between Lough Corrib and Lough Mask; the other to Cornamona, which served mainly as a pass-through for busloads of American tourists en route to *Quiet Man* country, where the Hollywood blockbuster was filmed with John Wayne and Maureen O'Hara in 1952. *Keep going, keep going*, I imagined the Cornamona locals whispering as the buses slowed down crossing over the bridge.

Coming over the final hill, Lough Corrib came fully into view and revealed her vastness. I was dumbstruck and spellbound. I was at the most northerly end of the lake and could look for miles down to the rugged waters, islands pock-marking its surface, ruins of cottages dotted across their fields. The scenery hinted at its rugged past, deep mysteries in her depths. Welcome to Corrib.

I saw the boats dotted across the water, their rods high in the air fishing and casting, and my heart raced a bit faster. How busy had their lines been this morning? I wondered in anticipation. I drove over the small bridge in the centre of Cornamona. A post office on the corner and pubs on either side were all that made up the commercial activity of the village. The real traffic was reserved for the boats on the water.

Cornamona may be on a road that is for passing through, destined for more famous, touristy environs, but it's a place that makes you stop, or at the very least slow down and look. Low hills creep up on one side of you, while the Maamturk mountains of Connemara stand tall in the distance. Stone walls and grey stone permeate the landscape, as they do all across the west of Ireland, but it's the water that dominates the village, the road and the scenery.

Boats are moored close by on the shore and in gardens outside houses and you can be sure the B&Bs and Tí Mháille's pub on the corner are dominated by fishing talk. Cornamona is a sleepy Irish by-water that comes alive at this time of year.

The shop and pub signs are all in Irish, as are the road signs, a reminder that you're deep in Connemara, deep in the Gaeltacht Irish-speaking Joyce country now. Hedgerows climb high and there's the occasional bungalow down a modest driveway, but what catches most of my attention is on the other side of the road. Only a stone's throw from me is Corrib. I can see the waters lapping against the shore, the soggy land meeting the lake's beginnings, a series of small enclaves as the land straddles the water.

There are four boats out on the lake that I can see. There's the tall, thin rods of those dapping – fishing with the live mayfly – or the swish-swish-swoosh of the fly angler casting back and forth over the waves, each singing their own hymn.

The waters aren't rough, but they're not flat calm either. The chilly breeze and dull, overcast conditions are putting a slight dampener on things. Only slightly, though. It's hard to be down when you're travelling with such high hopes for brown trout fishing on Corrib.

Driving another mile or so and I see the turn-off I've been looking for. The track continues on towards the lake, but I pull in to the right in front of a cosy stone cottage, nestled snugly off the road. I park, get out and stretch my tired body after nearly four hours' driving. I inhale fully, smelling the damp Connemara air, taking it deep into my lungs. It smells good, it smells fresh and clean. The door of the cottage is ajar and I walk towards it and knock.

'Come in, it's open,' calls the voice in an unmistakeable Galway accent.

Inside, it's warm and homely. It's a fly angler's home: photographs of fish, drawings of fish, fishing flies framed, antiques and trinkets to do with fly fishing, and a map of Corrib all adorn the walls of the open-plan kitchen-living room.

I'm in the house of Tom 'Doc' Sullivan, one of Corrib's most knowledgeable and respected guides, a Cornamona local and son of the local GP, Éamonn, hence the moniker Tom 'Doc', to differentiate him from all the other Sullivans in the area.

Introduced to fishing on the lake by his father when he was a boy, it captured his heart and soul and he has been guiding the waters and handling boats on his own since he was a teenager, about thirty years ago. He knows every rock, inlet and island better than the roads leading to his house probably. A hundred metres down the lane is his shed with his boats and gear, but first it's time for tea.

'Like any rural area, if you've anything going for you, you'll really plug for it,' he tells me as he puts the kettle on and I take a seat at the long wooden table. 'We're very lucky in Cornamona, the fishing has always been a boon to the area. There's a long tradition on Corrib of professional fishermen because of the availability of trout – between 1904 and 1912 something like 12 tonnes of trout were sold out of Lough Corrib. And that's the only official record you get of the lake because there's no fishing records as such. Then once they opened the railway line they were able to ship the fish to Billingsgate in London.'

In those days the season opened (and still does) on 1 February with the priest's blessing of the boats ceremony on the water's edge. They fished in punts, 12 feet in length with one set of oars. One pull of the oars would pull you 6 or 7 yards; they could row all day, and they had to, it was their livelihood. The set-up was three ash sticks hanging out with bells on the end. Hemp line was attached with minnows dangling enticingly in the water at the end. Bricíns they were called – Irish for 'little trout'.

The professional fishermen, Tom Doc explained, all came from the west side of the lake where Cornamona and Oughterard are situated, as Corrib lies between igneous granite rock to the west and the limestone plains on the east side.

Renowned local angler Paddy Summerville, who passed away in 2014 after a lifetime spent on Corrib, used to recount how they'd fish on the lake for the day by trolling – not fly fishing, mind, but trolling with a lure behind the boat, as this was for money. Fly fishing was for sport afterwards.

At the end of the day they would row across to Oughterard and then cycle into the village to put the fish on the train; the trout would be sold in Billingsgate the next morning, a fresh Irish brown trout not even a day out of the water. Receiving their money as the train pulled out, the fishermen would go to the pub for two or three pints before heading home, ready to do it all again the next morning.

'That's my London out there,' Paddy told Tom Doc once beside the shore, pointing out across the vast waters. 'That's why we never emigrated, that was my London.'

Ireland is the only country in Western Europe that has waters like this, a consequence of the morphology of the lakes, the geography of where Ireland is and the climate we have. The base rock is limestone: soft, so the water can dissolve through it and you end up with alkaline water, and with high levels of calcium and other salts which enable the plant life to grow – vital for the brown trout to thrive.

Huge populations of macroinvertebrates – shrimps, snails, insects – then colonise those weed beds and there's your trout food. There are lots of trout lakes in Norway and Sweden and Scotland, but most of those waters are too deep.

One of the reasons Corrib is a jewel in the crown of Irish waters is that it has a huge sub-catchment area with lots of big, shallow, fast-flowing rivers flowing into it from the surrounding countryside, places where the trout can reproduce. After they hatch, they spend anything from a couple of months to two years in the river nearby before they migrate downstream into Corrib until they mature before returning home to the same stream to spawn. It's perfect conditions for the thriving ecosystem and fishery that has continued in this vein for hundreds, if not thousands, of years.

In years past you could set the clock by 20 May when the first appearance of the white blooms of the mayflower along the ditches and shoreline would be the signal for what was to come. Right on cue, the mayfly hatch would be up and the trout would begin rising in substantial numbers that would see the start of the mayfly season with the arrival of the 'gents' coming from Dublin, Belfast, Scotland and England. Doctors, bank managers, businessmen; there was even an old ex-First World War naval captain who, when fishing, always stood on the boat no matter what the weather or how rocky the lake was. He never allowed himself to lose his sea-boots after all that time.

'The farm was neglected for the two or three weeks that the mayfly was up,' remembers Liam Sullivan (no relation to Tom Doc), who joined us for tea and whose family provided accommodation to visiting anglers since the early 1900s. 'My father always said he gave up growing a vegetable garden because you were never there during the mayfly season and that was when all the weeds grew.'

For Irish families, anglers or not, this was an opportunity to

earn extra income for those few weeks either through providing accommodation or ghillieing for the visitors, or with the kids selling live mayflies to the anglers. Families made the most of it while they could; entire communities were involved. It was an important time of year for these locals, not just for the professionals.

'It was a long, hard life here,' says Liam. 'Come nine o'clock it was bedtime as my mother would be up cutting bread in the morning before seven and the packed lunches had to be ready for the anglers and then they'd have dinner in the evening.

'There would be up to twenty guests at mayfly time and there was one family that came from Wales year after year, the Joneses. We even have a room upstairs called Joneses' Room because they always stayed in the same room. But in general, though, it was mainly Dublin people. My father always fished with Stackpole and Lawlor. Stackpole was a bank manager; Lawlor was a doctor. People couldn't afford to be taking holidays and fishing unless they had good jobs.'

Some are still coming as well, including a group affectionately known as 'the Dubliners' who have been visiting since the 1960s but their numbers are slowly dwindling and are now down to just two of the original group.

The Sullivans' guesthouse closed a number of years ago, the days of booking and spending weeks fishing long gone. Now a snatched weekend might be the height of it or else the option of fishing in far-flung places such as Iceland has provided an alternative. But for those few guests such as the Dubliners who are still coming for the mayfly, they keep the rooms ready, until the day they stop coming.

As long as the fishing remains strong, there will always be anglers coming to Corrib, but as the numbers and lengths of stay decline, it is the communities and villages such as Cornamona that are suffering.

As we finished our tea, Tom Doc's friend Eamonn Gavin called over. His mother was the postmistress of the village for over fifty years and he remembers the heyday of the festival.

'You'd notice the atmosphere alright,' he says. 'You'd drive along the Corrib shore and you'd see all the boats out there with maybe ten or fifteen boats in a row trying to get in on a drift. You'd often see five people in a boat dapping across the lake, chatting away, going for a big long lunch on the islands provided by the guesthouse, and fishing away again in the evening.

'I can remember families that all fished together: father, mother, children, aunts, uncles. They would hire out a couple of boats or would have a couple of local ghillies that they would bring out. In the post office itself there'd be a lot more phone calls and bookings, there'd be messages left, telegrams being sent saying "The mayfly is up" and other telegrams arriving saying, "We'll be there tomorrow." It happened that quickly. People would be on standby waiting for the mayfly. They'd be waiting. They could be in England, Scotland or Germany and as soon as the telegram arrived with those four words, "The mayfly is up", they'd be over.'

Eamonn's house was the central communications hub for the village – 'We were the internet of the time,' he says. The phone system would come on at eight o'clock in the morning linking up with Ballinrobe, which was the nearest exchange, and would remain on until ten o'clock at night, a constant ringing of bells in their daily lives.

'There were nine lines out and once we switched on the system in the morning, if somebody wanted to make a phone call, the phone would ring. We had bells throughout the house so we could hear it from anywhere and from the age of ten we were all trained in how to use it.

'The bell would ring and a little number would fall, say 101 dropped down, you'd put a little plug into that number and you'd say "Cornamona Post Office". The person would say, "I'd like to make a phone call to x, please," and you would take down the details. If they had a coin box you would say, "Please have your money ready," and it could be 30p or something like that for your three minutes.

'Then we would push a plug into the Ballinrobe socket and say, "Hi, Ballinrobe, this is Cornamona here, we want to make a trunk call to x, please, from Cornamona 101." Then they would say, "We'll ring you back in a few minutes, Cornamona," and you'd sit there and wait and eventually they'd ring back and say they were ready to put that call through. We would put the corresponding plug into the number and meanwhile the person is sitting at home waiting for you to ring back and have it hooked up.

'We grew up with bells going off in the house the whole time. We also took over the night service as well for a year and then we had it going for twenty-four hours, seven days a week. My mother had two days off in the year in all that time – Good Friday and Christmas Day.'

Remarkably, Cornamona was the second-last village in

Ireland to switch from a manual phone switchboard system to an automatic one, the change occurring only in 1986. Eamonn laughs and thinks back nostalgically to the antiquated system, a far cry from the instant communications of the internet and mobile phone these days, where anglers are now in the boat taking pictures and keeping friends updated in real time.

Yet 'the good old days' is the proverbial watch-cry of the angler, always muttered by generations gone past, and while there's a certain rose-tinted sepia in such talk, the reality is, from a fishing perspective, the numbers of fish being caught were much more prolific then. The boats would be coming in off the lake at day's end with twenty-plus fish; any wonder then that when the hatch was on, the line of cars would be pulling up in the morning impatient to start.

I hadn't driven from home just to hear about the history, however. There was only one way to experience the mayfly on Lough Corrib and after we finished the tea and stories in Tom Doc's house, we headed down to his shed where we tackled up and pulled our waders on. Before going out in the boat, though, in time-honoured fashion we had to try and collect the live mayflies on the shore.

'We are looking for mayfly that have hatched and blown right in towards the shore,' Tom explained. 'When the mayfly hits the shore, they climb onto the nearest rock to try and get a bit of shelter from the wind behind the rock. We're trying to look behind the rocks to pick them and put them into the mayfly box.

'There were once huge hatches of mayfly and it would take you a while to pick a full box of them but we would have them ready in the morning to sell to the visiting anglers. I remember when I started picking mayflies they were 50p a dozen and then it went up to £1 a dozen. There was inflation you see because it was supply and demand!'

Dapping isn't done as much nowadays and the scenes of kids skipping school to catch mayflies is a thing of the past, though you will still see the occasional, entrepreneurial ones out and about around Oughterard hoping to make a few extra euros.

In truth, the hatch of mayfly isn't as prolific as it once was either and dapping as a fishing method is becoming less popular, but some of the locals will still take out the dapping rods when conditions dictate. The beauty of dapping is you don't have to have the skill of fly casting. Find the live mayfly, attach it to the hook on the end of the dapping floss and out it goes, dancing on the water's surface, ideally with a bit of wind and a wave to help its movement.

But today, we were struggling to locate many mayflies, proving that modern hatches had reduced dramatically in recent years.

'The hatch isn't really on just yet but they are hatching,' Tom said optimistically, keeping the spirits up as a good guide does. 'We'll keep walking. Oh, there's one. Hold on. See him there behind the stone? And into the box he goes.'

We spent about thirty minutes walking along the shoreline picking out the odd few mayflies and it was more tedious and more difficult than I imagined. Under the warmth of the May sunshine you could easily see the attraction for schoolkids, but similarly, for the time-short angler who wants to be out on the water, it's easier to fly fish with artificial flies instead.

We had enough mayflies in the box by now and as we got

into the boat and pushed out onto the lake Tom Doc told me how, despite being sent to Dublin to boarding school, his heart was always in the countryside and fishing. Days in the classroom would be spent hiding fishing magazines from the teacher and as soon as the holidays arrived, he was on the train back to Galway, itching to spend the summer fishing on Corrib.

After studying business and marketing in college he was soon in the nine-to-five workplace but quickly realised it wasn't for him. He quit and went travelling around Europe without any real plan or goal in mind. He knew he didn't want to be stuck in an office, that just wasn't for him, but what *did* he want? That was the difficult question.

He was back home in Cornamona after his travels not doing much when Roy Peirce, the owner of Grasshopper Cottage, an angler's B&B down the road, called him. 'I've two guys who need a boatman tomorrow, would you do it?'

'I told him I would,' Tom Doc remembers. 'And that was my first introduction to guiding. I got a week that year, and the following year I bought my own boat and I had two weeks. Then gradually it went on from there and by 1999 I was getting so busy that I couldn't keep working in the local bar along with the guiding so in 2000 I went into it full-time.'

From March with the appearance of the duck fly at the beginning of the season right through to September and the end of the season, he had enough work to keep him going. Then in the off-season he would do fly-tying as well as beating on shoots with his three gundogs for some of the nearby estates on Delphi and Zetland.

Haunted by Waters

Tom Doc's life of spending most days on the water came to a sudden end with the 2007 recession when work was not as plentiful as before. So he reluctantly put the boat into dry dock for more regular work elsewhere, getting a job as a regional sales manager on the road.

'When I was driving away from Corrib in the morning and I was away I missed it, yeah. I'd be stuck in a car and on occasion would be nine hours in the car in a day.'

It was no surprise then that after six years on the road, he was aching to be back out doing the lake fishing and guiding again. As the economy started to pick up once more, he made the leap away from the steady income to return to the life he loved.

He's back where he belongs now, in his boat on Lough Corrib helping people to catch brown trout, though he admits things are not the same. The recession has had a ripple effect on the fly fishing economy that it's still struggling to recover from while cheap flights have brought far-flung destinations closer to hand and easier to reach.

As the numbers of visiting anglers has dropped off, it's not just the guides who are feeling the effects; there are others, from the publican to the restaurant and the local B&B owner, who have felt it too.

Peter O'Reilly, one of Ireland's most renowned fly fishermen, who was famous for his invaluable books detailing the loughs and rivers of Ireland, was also a regular to Corrib down through the years, fishing and giving courses out of Oughterard.

'Every trout fisher has heard of Corrib,' he recalled of the glory days of fishing during the mayfly hatch on the lough. 'It's out there and there's the fascination, the desire, wondering, "Someday I wonder will I ever be able to fish there?" And for most people things fall into place, they meet up with a friend who has already been, they get an invitation and they go and fish and of course as soon as they catch a fish they've got the bug.

'Corrib had everything, from the numbers of fish to the mayfly hatch. You would hear stories of the trout giving themselves up during this time. They said the schoolteachers went mitching and the judges abandoned their benches to go fishing during the mayfly. And it really was true. I met a schoolteacher who told me he was teaching close by and said if he had a free class he would go down to the lake and fish.'

Key to it all is getting out onto the water and experiencing the thrill of dapping, fly fishing and indeed any other type of fishing. Once you feel that bend in the rod and land your first fish then you are indeed 'hooked'. When you try to explain it to a non-angler you get quizzical looks, people unable to understand how or why it can be so enticing. While some people hit a ball into a hole, or others watch birds, fishing ignites a passion and a feeling that only anglers can understand. But it's also more than that.

'Many men go fishing all of their lives without knowing that it is not fish they are after,' wrote Thoreau.

For me, and for many others, there is a yearning to be in nature, to be still. Fishing offers an escape from life's hectic schedule, the chance to break free of it all and live life to its fullest. And today on Corrib, there are no work calls or emails on my phone to intrude on my day.

It was time for me to catch a fish, to feel that bend from a

Corrib trout, though the howling gales and squally waves as we drove out across the lake told us it was going to be anything but easy. These were far from the mayfly conditions I had envisaged but Tom soon identified a drift and, cutting the engine, the boat gently followed the lapping waters where we hoped some trout could be tempted to take our mayflies on the dap.

With the 15-foot rod sticking out over the water and a mayfly on the end of the line, I held the rod high, almost vertical, and watched as the wind began to blow the dapping line over the water like a sail, dangling it enticingly for any fish looking up.

'Let the fly dance on top of the wave,' Tom instructed. 'That's it. Now drop the rod a bit, put the butt of the rod in towards your hip. Yeah, that's it. Has the fly landed on the water yet?'

I could see the mayfly struggling in the water, certain that at any moment the jaws of a wild trout would come up from the deep and engulf it.

'You've got to keep it on top of the water. That's it. But here's the thing, you can't have too much line. This is the little skill that comes into it, it's knowing when the breeze gets stronger and is about to push the fly off, to drop the rod, and accordingly, when the wind is decreasing, to lift the rod. It's like the spinnaker sail at the front of a yacht, that's what you want.'

It's a fine balance to get the technique right. The line goes out in the wind, carrying the fly forward. Trying to maintain the tension, it's easy to forget that you're also watching for a fish to take the fly. Quite often a fish's method of taking the fly is he'll drown it first and then he'll come back and eat it. There are other occasions when the fish is taking it, he's not splashing, he's just sucking it in gently, but you have to be slow in your strike.

'It's happened – strike, lift her out and strike!'

Tom Doc's voice intruded suddenly on my thoughts. I struck but was too late.

'Damn it, he's gone!'

'Gone? That would've been a nice fish. There was a very gentle take, I just happened to see it and I gave you three seconds but …'

I had felt a little something, though maybe it was just the water lapping, I don't know. But that was as close as we got. One missed rise. Soon afterwards the hatch died off for the day while the wind and rain kept up relentlessly.

Hard to believe we were at the end of May and although the white buds of the mayflower were trying to bloom, and there were some mayflies hatching, the conditions were dire and the fish weren't biting.

On shore I helped Tom pull in the boat, and we met others coming back from the water as well. It was the same for them all: poor conditions and poor fishing. I couldn't help but think about what I had been told by anglers and scientists alike – that with the changing weather patterns, the changing environment, and the overall effects on the fishing and number of visitors, it's true, the mayfly fishing isn't what it once was.

But there would be other days. The other anglers were hopeful the weather would be better tomorrow and the fishing would pick up. Good days will follow. The angler is the eternal optimist – you have to be – otherwise your rods would be put away and never taken out again. I felt refreshed and rejuvenated as I returned to my car to begin the long drive home. Life's stresses and strains had been left behind for a day, and although work problems and new deadlines would still be waiting for me when I got home, I had a new energy to tackle them face-on. I would be back on the 06.15 train to Dublin the next morning but I would have the experience of today to reflect upon. The mayfly ended its life exhausted and spent after just twenty-four hours but I at least had many more days ahead. I might have had no fish, but the magic of Lough Corrib had stirred my heart and I would be back for more than a day.

6.

*Tipperary
Days*

The early-season promise was well and truly forgotten, the expected summer conditions never materialising. The heatwave of 2018 was not going to be reappearing in 2019, it seemed. Rain showers, blustery winds and cool evenings marked the days into June and people, anglers especially, were grumbling in spades about it, looking up at the foreboding skies in despair.

I hadn't been out fishing since my unsuccessful trip to Corrib and I was at a low ebb. The thrill after my time on Corrib had got lost under the pressures of work and new deadlines looming. Strangely, when time away fishing is what I need most to help give me perspective and a chance for self-reflection, I find it hardest to drag myself out to the river. It's as if the fog of work becomes so engulfing that you can't see a way out. I read somewhere that if you don't have time for thirty minutes of exercise or meditation, that's when you need sixty minutes instead. A fishing trip to Delphi which I had planned for months had to be cancelled due to a family illness. Then I had to cancel en route to the Blackwater when a last-minute work schedule was changed.

But sometimes in your lowest moments you need to push yourself out of your comfort zone. All you know is that out there, not far away, is the water, and that's where you want to be.

This time it took my seven-year-old to push me there. We were to spend some quality time together when he mentioned fishing to me, remembering I had promised it when the weather got better. Today there was a break in the clouds, the sun was finally shining and I had a young boy with excited eyes looking up at me.

'Okay, let's do it,' I told him and in less than two minutes flat he was packed and ready at the door. 'Like to see you get ready for school that quick,' I teased him. 'Here, don't forget this.' It was a fishing cap, but not just any – it was the one Ryan had got on our first ever fishing trip together a year ago, which happened to be in Brooklyn's Prospect Park.

Now it's a year later and myself and Ryan pack the car for Ardaire Springs. It's an artificial lake set in the fields outside Mooncoin in south Kilkenny, a put-and-take fishery that wouldn't normally be my cup of tea when it comes to fly fishing, but for young kids it's a great way to fish. With large rainbow trout swimming right up to the edge of the water, it gets a seven-year-old's heart pumping in excitement, and even my forty-one-year-old heart as well.

Ryan couldn't believe his eyes. The rainbow trout were making leaps showing off their colours of silver, red and blue as if trying to escape the water right in front of us. 'Look at that fish!' he screamed out. 'And another one! Over there! Dad, did you see that one?' His excitement and enthusiasm was infectious.

We settled into a relaxing rhythm. Ryan chose the fly, which I tied on; he chose which fish I should cast to and then I handed him the rod to slowly strip in the line to try and entice the fish to take it. Every other cast I'd have a go, and then when he was starting to get bored I'd get him to pick another fly.

Holding the rod and pulling the line in, mixing up the speed, it was easy for him and sometimes, unconsciously, as the fly came close to the bank Ryan would do a roll cast and flick the line out ahead of him. I had never taught him any fly fishing casts before and I was astonished to see him just do it naturally as if it was the most normal thing in the world. Kids don't overthink things, show them something new and they just jump right in without worrying about doing it perfectly; they're in the moment every time, enjoying it for what it is.

An angler to our left, fishing with worms, had just caught a nice 3-lb rainbow and Ryan was wondering why we couldn't do the same. The pressure was on. The casting was going well, there was a strong breeze behind us and we were within range of the cruising fish. But they still weren't interested. I opted for a slow sinker but that still wasn't working. Then I decided to try a floater and Ryan said I should try 'that yellow fly there in the corner'. It was some sort of woolly bugger, aptly loud and non-descript but hadn't been on the advised list of flies that had been catching fish. What had we got to lose, though? When in doubt, always go with the seven-year-old's advice.

As soon as the fly landed, a fish attacked it and we only missed it because I struck too quickly. I re-cast immediately and again the fly was attacked in the first few seconds. I struck more calmly and this time we were in. 'You've got a fish, Ryan,' I told his unbelieving ears. The bend in the rod was enough to convince him of the size of the fish and I handed him the rod. 'Your turn now.' He reeled it in slowly but as the fish went on one of its early runs, the rod nearly fell from Ryan's hands and I caught it just in time. 'You take it, Dad – I want to net it!'

I got it to the bank in a few minutes and Ryan was able to slide the net into the water to catch the fish. His day was made, as was mine. The hook was removed and pictures quickly taken of Ryan's first rainbow trout of about 2½ lbs. We put the fish back into the water and he swam free. We caught another fish in the afternoon, but it didn't get any better than that first one and I could tell Ryan's attention was drifting so we reeled in to head home.

That evening, the kids had gone to bed and I was suddenly feeling relaxed again. 'It's taken years off your face,' my wife told me and I said I'd take that as a compliment.

It was the weekend, the clock in the kitchen ticked past 8.30 p.m. and I would normally be putting my feet up, reading and relaxing with a glass of wine watching the setting sun. That was too easy, I decided. Why not try something different instead? 'I'm heading down to the river,' I told Trina suddenly.

I jumped in the car, where my rod and trout bag were still in the boot from earlier, and drove off without even going to the shed for my waders; I didn't want anything to get in the way of my impulse, afraid it might be stopped if anything slowed it down or was put in its way.

Pulling out of the house and driving down the road is usually when I decide what part of the river I'm going to fish. Ballybrado is only five minutes away but also usually the busiest, which is why, most of the time, I find myself driving on upstream for some fishing solitude.

Not this evening, though. I just wanted to be on the river quickly, without thinking, and to hell if there were lots of people there, just go with it, I said to myself. My wife was right, the fishing in Ardaire had done something for me alright. The stress of the last few weeks of work had dissipated in the few hours spent with Ryan.

The evening was calm and mild, though without much heat as I drove slowly down the grass-grown track that leads to the Suir. This time last year we were in the midst of one of the longest droughts on record; now we were having to cope with wind and rain in June.

As I turned the last corner at the bottom of the track I could see there were no other parked cars, which meant there were no other anglers on the beat. I had the place to myself. I parked the car, got out and opened the boot. What would it be this evening? Dry fly, I decided; yes, time for my first dry fly fishing of the season. It was June and I had missed the best of the mayfly on the river, and though the evening was still a bit dull for much of a rise, it had never stopped me before.

With my wellies on and 5-weight rod in hand, I headed on upstream to be away from any late arrivals. There was only the occasional splosh of a rising fish and sporadic ripples here and there across the river, but I was still hopeful it would pick up.

For the first hour I had no takers, my dry fly skills still rudimentary in terms of reading the rises and the currents. Still, though, if you can hit it right with some sort of general attractor pattern, you can still have some incredible fishing.

Then just before 10 p.m., just as it's beginning to get dark, a button is switched on and the river comes alive with rising trout. One of the great wonders of nature is to see the water in full abandon with brown trout sploshing, slurping and plopping their way to feasts of flies on the water's surface. It's a magical sight that stirs the emotions and senses and I changed fly hurriedly before realising I was all out of floatant. It was the one thing needed to keep the fly afloat on the water for the fish to take and I also needed to see its white post in the fading light.

I'd just have to make do, I figured, and see if I could dry the fly with some mid-air casts and hope the drifts would be short enough to keep it on the surface for those few seconds. I walked along the bank spotting a few rises mid-stream that looked promising. I stopped and pulled some line from the reel before casting out over the reeds to a rising fish. The 15-foot leader landed gently mid-stream and even though I couldn't see the fly in the darkening light it didn't matter, I felt the weight of the world sink away standing there casting to rising fish.

Then all changed. As I tracked the end of my fly line past square and downstream there was the unmistakeable sight of the line being pulled suddenly under and a circular ripple in the water a few feet above where my fly would have been.

Instinctively I struck, lifting the rod high above me and yes, I was in! A trout was on. Not just any trout, I realised, but something big. He immediately dived deep and headed for the middle of the flow before somersaulting into the air. The splash and ripples as he landed created bow-waves across the now-quiet pool.

I try to get the fish under control but he's headed downstream and I follow, trying to gain line all the time, gradually winning the battle before he shoots off again with more somersaults in the process. I'm speechless but caught in the moment and the excitement.

Slowly I start to gain control and now had to think about landing the fish and somehow getting it closer to the water's edge. While the banks are beautifully wild with ample space for a back cast and just reeds in front to deal with, I was still up on a bank above the river wearing only wellingtons. Going into the river wasn't an option without my waders and as I pulled my net out, I noticed the spring mechanism on it was broken. Cursing my luck, the net was ditched while I kept the tension on, looking desperately for somewhere I could get closer to the water without giving myself a ducking.

There were reeds below me; tall reeds so thick I couldn't quite make out if they were directly in the river or merely on muddy ground which, at least, wouldn't be as deep (or so I hoped). This was a good fish, I knew it, maybe a personal best, and I was willing to do whatever was needed to land it.

So I took a leap of faith and jumped into the reeds, expecting to be getting a dunking at any moment. But no, thankfully, they catch my fall, precariously holding me just out of the river and inches above the water. I can't move now but it doesn't matter, I can at least reach out to grab the leader and land the fish myself.

It's under my control now and despite one last somersault for freedom I'm able to inch him closer and closer within my grasp. His mouth is out of the water, the hook holding firm in the corner. I grab hold of the leader and swing the fish in over the reeds, praying it will all stay on. My luck holds as does the leader and I dive down on my knees to grab the magnificent trout lying before me on top of the reed bed.

It's an incredible fish, close to 4 lbs. Probably 3½ lbs in all truth but my heart was seeing 4 lbs. I couldn't believe it. I was shaking with the excitement of the hunt, managing to actually bring him to hand and here he is now before me: the most perfect specimen of brown trout I had ever caught, brown spots and a golden hue glistening along the length of his body. I measure him against my rod from the butt upwards, seeing in disbelief his tail go past the keeper ring and near to the first rod ring. It's a phenomenal fish in any book, especially mine, and it's the biggest brown trout I have ever caught.

Quickly I take out my phone, a basic Nokia type that I have been using for the last few days as my iPhone was broken and in need of repair. It's a small, handheld and robust phone about half the size of an iPhone which takes about ten minutes to send a text. I'm missing my iPhone but still, there's been something liberating about only being able to text and make calls on this basic Nokia. I was becoming a bit of a Luddite and I was actually quite alright with that.

Until now. This moment, the greatest of my fly fishing life so far, and the phone is dead. I stare in disbelief and disgust at this ancient relic in my hand and think briefly of chucking it into the river. If only I'd had my iPhone, my trusty smartphone that has recorded so many of my catches down through the years and that remain safe in the cloud. What's worse, I had glanced at the battery life on the Nokia before heading out and seeing one bar on it, thought, 'Should be fine'. It's not as if I had been using it in the ninety minutes I had been on the river, but regardless, it was dead and now there would be no crowning glory for me.

No saving the photo as my screensaver, no showing the kids,

no boastful 'See, this is why I go fishing' to my wife who always wonders about me returning empty-handed each time. No picture to join the gallery in looking back at my fishing seasons. This was just me, here on my knees in the reeds in my wellies, mucky and damp with the finest brown trout I have ever caught.

A slap of his tail brings me back to the moment. This guy needs to get back into the water. For a second I think how splendid he would look in a glass case behind my desk. Since I couldn't get a photo, would a stuffing be the next best thing? No, I can't. I've always put back any trout I've caught and this guy deserves to go back, for his size, his fight, his somersaults, and the pounding excitement he has given me.

Landing him, without a net, in my wellies, is enough for me. As I hold him in the water to recover, I realise I'm shaking inside with the thrill. Then, with a kick he's gone, back into the depths of the river. I clean my hands in the cold water, pick up my rod and shake my head in disbelief once more before clambering back up the bank.

Incredibly, the rises were still going on around me. I'd been oblivious to it all as soon as I had hooked the trout but quickly my attention turned back to the feeding going on. I cast out again, the same fly floating mid-stream, and again, incredibly, it's sucked down. I lift the rod and again I'm into a decent-sized fish. I can't believe my luck. But this time it doesn't hold on and within seconds the line comes loose and the fish is gone.

At least I had my previous success, this lost fish is just a regular tale in terms of my Suir fishing. The one that did stay on, the one that I did land, now that's a better story to tell. Just a pity people will have to take my word for it. I reel in and call it a night. Dusk has set in, it's nearly 10.30 p.m. and I walk across the fields to my car, a feeling of utter happiness and peace that I hadn't felt in a long time. The worries of these last few weeks of work have melted away, healed by an unexpected evening beside the river.

7.

Connemara Jewels

*T*he year is passing. The summer solstice has arrived, bringing with it the longest day of the year. It's a time for bright evenings and the hope of the summer to come. Traditionally Saint John's Eve on 23 June was marked by bonfires and blessings, prayers for the crops and good luck and it also marked the arrival of the salmon and sea trout runs. Boats and nets would be blessed, while for the anglers, silent prayers would be said for abundant fishing.

The tradition of villages lighting bonfires and gathering for music, dancing and games has all but died out now and all we have are the writings from long-dead authors recounting their experiences of the festivities in the nineteenth and early twentieth centuries.

'Last night was St John's Eve, and bonfires – a relic of Druidical rites – were lighted all over the country, the largest of all being in the town square of Belmullet, where a crowd of small boys shrieked and cheered and threw up firebrands for hours together,' John Millington Synge wrote of a visit in 1905, while W.B. Yeats, who was with him, recalled a little girl in the crowd, in an ecstasy of pleasure and dread, clutching Synge by the hand and standing close in his shadow until the fiery games were over.

Now, though, the turning points of the seasons are just more numbered days on the calendar but I intend to mark this one my own way as I drive to Connemara to celebrate the beginning of the grilse salmon run. Like New Year's Day on the Drowes, 1 February on the Blackwater, or Saint Patrick's Day on the Suir, I find myself drawn to nature's changes in our calendar year. The summer solstice and winter solstice are two more dramatic dates, carrying the sense that we're witnessing a change into something new.

Driving to Connemara for the summer salmon in the wake of the summer solstice and Saint John's Eve, I'm in the footsteps once more of what Irish people have been doing for hundreds, if not thousands, of years.

I had managed to squeeze my work to get it all done by Thursday and now had Friday free. I was taking the day off for myself and setting off at the crack of dawn to go fishing in one of those places I had long read about. I was as excited as I had been on my New Year's Eve trip to the Drowes.

Ballynahinch Castle is one of those fairytale fisheries you tell people about. An hour west of Galway, you turn off the Clifden road under the watching Twelve Bens mountains and enter a private, secluded, pristine and intimate estate. I fell in love with it the first time I fished there courtesy of my wife and a fortieth birthday present two years earlier.

During that visit I had caught a few small sea trout and brown trout and was smitten with the fishery, the castle and the solitude. From the breakfast table or on an evening walk you could see salmon leaping in the Ballynahinch River that flowed right next to the building and on that first trip I decided I would come back and see what the fishery really had to offer.

It's a fly angler's home from home, a place where you can walk

into the bar with your waders dripping and fly rod left by the door, surrounded by casts of 20 lb salmon and 10 lb trout hanging on the wall. There were also shelves of books, photos and flies, and some of the books caught my attention.

There were the usual fly fishing books from the likes of Kingsmill Moore and Roderick Haig-Brown but there were also titles on English cricket and on Indian monarchs. Cricket I could perhaps understand but Indian princes?

Like so many places in Connemara, Ballynahinch has had a long and varied history. It was originally just one of the many castles the ruling O'Flaherty clan held between Galway and Mayo and their hold on the land was further cemented when the celebrated 'pirate queen' Grace O'Malley married into the family in 1546.

When her husband Donal died Grace became head of the household, ruling with a strength of will matched only by Queen Elizabeth I, and indeed the two female rulers came face to face in a famous meeting in 1593, conversing only in Latin, an event that marked Grace as the only Gaelic woman ever to appear in the court of the British monarchy.

However, by then, the O'Flahertys' influence and independence was waning and in the 1700s it was the Martin family, who had first arrived with Strongbow in 1169 and established themselves as one of the fourteen tribes of Galway, that was to take control of Ballynahinch into the nineteenth century.

The house was extensively renovated in 1813 when it became the principal seat of the Martin family, friends to the prince regent, who was later to become King George IV. Daniel

O'Connell stayed a night en route to a repeal meeting in Clifden, while English novelist William Thackeray wrote about it with an early reference to fly fishing on the fishery:

> O you who laboriously throws flies in English Rivers, and catch at the expiration of a day's walking casting and wadeing two or three feeble little trout of two or three ounces in weight, how you would rejoice to have but one hour's sport on Derryclare or Ballynahinch; where you have but cast, and lo! A big trout springs to your fly.

The Berridge family were the next owners of the estate and enlarged the castle to what it is today before it was sold to His Highness the Maharaja Jam Sahib of Nawanager, better known as Ranjitsinhji, or Ranji Prince of Cricketers, in 1924. Not your average Anglo-Irish landlord or one of the Galway tribes you might imagine.

Tales are told of the prince arriving into Galway every summer where he would purchase five new motorcars, two limousines and three smaller cars. Returning to England in October, he would then donate the cars to the local parish priest to be sold for the parish's benefit. He would even have his own railway carriage to take him from Galway to the Ballynahinch station and upon his arrival locals would light firecrackers along the line to welcome him. Such was his lavish lifestyle and spending, it was no wonder that debt issues plagued the prince in England and India for a lot of his life.

He died suddenly on 1 April 1932, having sampled the Connemara salmon fishing on the estate for only eight seasons, but his legacy to the Ballynahinch fishery is all around, from the walkways to the fishing piers and huts that are still in use today. There's not many places you can say that you've fished in the footsteps of an Indian prince.

When the Irish Tourist Board took possession of the estate in 1946, it was the first time that the salmon fishing was available to the public after centuries of being privately held. Éamon de Valera was one of the first visitors as was Liam O'Flaherty the writer and Alec Guinness the actor.

It passed once again into private hands in the 1950s and in the decades since has seen celebrities, prime ministers and even a US president, Gerald Ford, pay a visit. Most of the visitors stop only briefly in the castle for a short stay as part of their tours of Connemara, so it leaves more of the fishing to the fly anglers who yearn for the peace and quiet that it offers.

Ballynahinch and Connemara is an enchanting place and has entranced anglers for a long time. Aside from the landscape that is dotted with hundreds of lakes and rivers where you could spend a lifetime trying to fish all of its waters, there is a romantic appeal to the region as well. Castles, lodges and country estates lie across the different valleys, each one with its own history and link to the past. The black and white photos of anglers from times past only tell some of the story but the next generation fishes in their footsteps, carrying on the fly fishing tradition.

I travelled in hope. For the last two weeks rain had been sparse but on this Sunday they were predicting rain and even spot flooding. All salmon anglers pray for some rain to bring the salmon in off the tide, and in the days afterwards as the river settles down in height it is a prime time for catching them. Time it right and you can be into some incredible fishing. Too much rain and the river might be flooded and your chances of a fish dimmed.

This morning, as I reached Tipperary Town by 6.30 a.m., the first showers began to fall and the rain got steadily heavier the further north and west I travelled.

I arrived into the grounds of Ballynahinch just after 9 a.m. with the grey clouds hanging low and ominous-looking over the mountains surrounding the estate. I knew from past experience this was not a good sign and sure enough, as I walked into the castle to confirm my booking, one of the waiting ghillies confirmed as much. 'The rain is welcome alright, but arra, those clouds are too low, they need to push on or they'll put the fish off.'

You don't have much choice about the clouds when you've driven for three hours, however, and Greg, the facilities manager and an ebullient Aussie, was giving out licences and permits with a positive air. He highlighted likely taking spots on the map of the river and wished me good luck.

The summer floods might come after Saint John's Day, but does that herald the arrival of the fish as it used to? Someone once said to me that the best salmon anglers are the richest ones as they could afford to fly off to Russia and Iceland where the salmon runs are vast. The rest of us have to make do, and unlike brown trout fishing where if you have an hour to spare you can head off to the river in the expectation of landing some fish, be

Haunted by Waters

it from nymph, wet or dry fly, to catch a salmon you have to put in the time with hours on the river.

But for me, time is a precious commodity. Between work, kids and family, the chance to give up days in pursuit of salmon is rare. It sometimes feels like life is passing me by. One minute you're just out of college with a life of excitement and potential ahead of you and the next you're in your forties with a mortgage, bills and a family, no longer as carefree or free-spirited. You have to be able to put in the time to chase and catch salmon, accept the many blank days that will come and be there at the right time when the river is coming into order. If you're standing on the river enough times, eventually the conditions will come good for you. Salmon fishing is a bit like life, perhaps: keep turning up and things will turn your way.

Or sometimes you can just get lucky, like two years earlier when I had a spare morning from work and paid a visit to the Blackwater down the motorway from me. There had been significant rainfall the previous week and the river's height was perfect. As I turned the bend on the Kilmurry beat and looked down to the island facing into the magnificent straight of river before me, there were fish leaping everywhere.

I hurried my steps, especially as I was the only angler on the beat. I couldn't believe my eyes as I clambered down the ladder and stood in amazement in the knee-deep water. Salmon were leaping right across the river, from the far bank to mid-flow and even right around me. They were fresh grilse come in off the tide a few hours earlier and they were in an excited mood.

And then a salmon leaped about a foot to my left. Bloody

hell. 'If I can't catch a fish today, I swear to God I'm taking up golf,' I muttered to myself as I stripped out line from my reel.

I cast out, for once in expectation and not just hope. It wasn't a case of knowing the lies, it was a case of casting out to one of the many fish leaping all around, and then on my second cast, mid-swing, came the unmistakeable and definite pull on the line. I let go of the loop in my left hand and watched the top of the rod as the pull became more definite. Now was the time. I lifted the rod up and felt the resistance of the fish. Yes, I was into a salmon.

The line shot off across and downstream and I let him go for a moment. Then I started reeling-and-giving, reeling-and-giving to try and coax him in. A few more runs were made, each less powerful than before though and I knew he was tiring. I had no net with me of course (the bent frame of my gye net hung useless in the shed at home) and I waded back to the bank to find a shallow stretch to land this precious first salmon of the season.

The fight had gone from him now and I pulled the leader easily in. There was a 5 lb silver grilse to marvel at fresh in off the tide with sea lice still on his flank. I struggled to get my phone out but managed to take a picture and then eased him back into the water, kicking off with his tail to rejoin the other salmon somewhere nearby. It was a wonderful, exhilarating experience I would take home with me and savour, a feeling of wholeness, of things coming right that would stay with me beyond the river.

I didn't have long to reflect on my first fish of the season though. Another splash nearby reminded me that the fish were still jumping. Where there's one there's another, I had been told, and get your fly back in the water again quickly.

Over the next ninety minutes, two more salmon were landed (and released), the best a 7 lb beauty, while another was lost 10 yards from the bank. And the entire time the salmon continued to jump right across the river. Some anglers can go entire seasons without that pull on the line but to have three fish in an hour and a half was incredible.

This was the 'red-letter day' anglers talk about and one that I would be talking about for the next few seasons until the right time and place came around once again. How long I would have to wait I didn't know, and it would depend on how often I could put myself on the river. But I had experienced it; I had the day that would make up for the blanks. That's what fishing is all about, storing up the memories of those days for when you're not catching, wondering if you'll ever catch again, providing the hope that the 'next cast' is what counts. One foot in front of the other becomes one cast after another.

And it wasn't even a day – barely two hours had passed before I reluctantly had to reel in and leave the river to return home. I climbed up the ladder with a heavy heart and as I turned my back on the pool walking back upstream to my car, I could still hear the splashes taunting me on the water behind.

That was then and this was now, the rain drizzling down as I walked through the woodlands of Ballynahinch Castle towards the first beat at the top of the river beside the lake. My hood was up and I was wondering what my chances would be like for the day.

The last time I was here, with the family, I struggled with a gusting wind, so much so, in fact, that I even managed to hook my top lip in the first thirty minutes of fishing. As I swung my rod from left to right, sweeping the line up, I must have decided to change the direction of the cast and crossed myself, pulling the anchor point and hook closer to me. As I cast forwards, I felt a sudden, sharp shock into my upper lip. For a moment I didn't have a clue what had happened. You go from preparing to watch the fly land on the water, to shouting out in pain at the hook now embedded into your lip.

Dealing with the pain is the first thing, what to do with your rod and line is the next. You don't want to drop it and have the line and hook pull at your skin, but all you want is to get the bloody hook out and see how much damage has been done.

Luckily I had a guide with me at the time. He was quickly over and took hold of the line and rod, taking the tension off. Now, in the middle of the pain I just felt embarrassed and all I could think of was, 'I haven't travelled all this way to have my day finished after thirty minutes through my own stupidity.'

'What will I do?' asked the young guide nervously.

'Why, take the f***ing thing out, of course!'

'Jesus, it's embedded deep,' he said as he dared take a closer look.

I could taste the blood dripping down from my lip and into my mouth and was spitting it out with difficulty, trying to keep it off my waders and jacket – I was still only concerned about fishing the rest of the day and was picturing myself walking into the bar covered in blood, a hook embedded into my mouth, just waiting to be mounted in a case alongside the other specimens.

'Just see what you can do,' I told him through gritted teeth.

'I'm not going to a doctor, I don't want to waste any more time with this.'

With shaking hands – not a comforting sight, but I didn't have much of a choice – he took hold of the hook. He cut the leader off so at least the tension was gone from that end. Then he grabbed the gape of the hook – thankfully it was a barbless single – and with his other hand held my top lip firmly.

'No messing around now,' I told him sternly. 'One shot at it, I don't care how much I scream or squirm, just one push and get it out.'

I could hear his quick intake of breath and the next moment I could feel the hook being pushed up and out – finally it was free.

'F**k me that's sore,' I shouted, spitting out more blood from the open cut. But the hook was out and the pain would go soon enough.

'You sure you don't want it looked at up in the castle or in the village?' the guide asked me, handing me the blood-stained hook.

'No, no, it will be fine. I can feel it's not too deep,' I replied as I felt the edges of the cut with my tongue. Once the bleeding stopped I knew I'd be back in business.

'Let's take a five-minute break.'

'Good idea,' I said, and sat on a rock on the edge of the river, still feeling like an idiot but also relieved that it hadn't been too serious and I could go on fishing with the minimum of fuss. Thankfully there were no other anglers around to see the right mess I had inflicted on myself.

'And best if we keep this to ourselves, especially in the bar,' I reminded him.

'Yes, of course,' came the reply, but I knew it would be the first topic amongst the guides at lunch. Well, maybe it had to happen sometime, and this was just my time, I thought ruefully.

I fished on for the rest of the day, albeit a bit tender in the mouth, but otherwise all was normal – no fish landed, so nothing out of the ordinary there. For the afternoon session (on the poetically named 'Beat 6'), and with this stretch of the river to myself, I was happy to explore all likely taking spots. Despite a few fish showing, my total was still zero, though the day was saved from a complete blank in the last hour before dinner when at the bottom pool I landed two small sea trout in fast water. At least it was a bend in the rod and I got to hold fish and release them back into the water.

That evening I re-joined Trina and the kids where we sat in the castle bar surrounded by the glass cases of trophy salmon and trout.

Anglers have a completely different mindset these days about catch and release. Smartphones at least have meant pictures have replaced dead fish as mementoes of memorable catches.

Two years later and I was now standing by the headwaters of the river. I crossed the footbridge to fish from the other bank. The wooden walkways to enable easy casting without getting into the river were a throwback to a bygone era of gentlemen anglers and Indian princes, but I still preferred to get my legs in the water, feel it lapping around my knees and plant my feet firmly on the riverbed. I wanted to get a better sense of the river and its mood by wading and casting from it.

The water wasn't cold, but the downpours, increasing in

intensity as the morning went on, started to seep through the sleeves and under the cuffs of my rain jacket. With my hood up, it made for unlikely summer grilse fishing. All I could see was the rain splashing onto the river in front of me.

I cast to likely spots, alternating between square and downstream casts, changing flies to micro trebles, occasional hitches, and the usual shrimps, collie dogs and sunrays. I was trying everything but not getting anywhere. The fly would swing through without a touch and I'd start again.

Still though, I wasn't despairing. This stretch of the fishery was intimate and soulful. Whereas downstream the river is open and the landscape rocky and sparse, here the trees crowded over me, the high banks gave a privacy and the pools cried out to be fished through. The river was only 30 feet or so in width and ravine-like in its surroundings.

I was relishing it, hopping from rocks to shingles, finding a likely spot to steady myself before casting the fly out. The casting was easy, and sometimes you even had to be careful not to overshoot the line, but even if you did, you could feather it as it hit the rockface on the far bank and watch the fly land tantalisingly in the water before swinging around.

I came to one particular spot that I knew would be worth a few casts. The river flowed into a slow pool that widened out with a high rock behind it and I could just imagine fish holding up there before waiting for the next flood. Looking downstream all I could see was a narrowing of the river as it reached the bridge and the road for the castle.

As the fly swung around – *zip* – it was taken and I watched the line straighten out, but knew from the pace of the take and the light pull that it wasn't a salmon. Sure enough as I lifted the rod, there was very little pressure on it and I was able to reel in a sea trout of ½ lb.

The rain kept pouring down and I could feel the damp soaking through to my t-shirt now. It was getting close to lunchtime when the fishing beats switched around.

I wondered how other anglers were faring and wasn't surprised when I sat up at the bar in the castle at lunchtime and was told no one else had caught a salmon that morning.

I lapped up the surroundings, with the buzz of eager anglers and curious tourists all around me. The fire blazed in the room, even though it was summer, giving it a peaty smell while busloads of American tourists arrived on day trips travelling around Connemara, bemused and some slightly taken aback by the sight of the fish on the walls when they first walked in. But then they saw the picture of former US president Gerald Ford and his wife Betty behind the bar and they gravitated towards it, smiling that someone familiar had also once been here.

I finished my coffee, anxious to get back out to the water for the afternoon and see if my luck had changed. However, it remained fruitless as I fished in front of the castle itself and I soon headed downstream to see what else the river had to offer. Each time it was in vain. I was still dripping wet and knew I'd be packing up soon to hit the road.

There are so many salmon fishing jewels in Connemara that it's hard to know where to begin or end. A wealthy benefactor or a very understanding wife, a healthy bank balance and a summer

Haunted by Waters

house near Maam Cross would probably be the ideal, from where you could set off each day, choosing which of the many fisheries were fishing well.

Within a short drive of each other there's the Rivers Erriff and Kylemore; Loughs Inagh and Screebe; Costello and Fermoyle Fisheries and of course Lough Corrib itself, and within the fisheries themselves there's innumerable loughs as well. There's so many for the fly angler to choose from and I'm envious of the days long gone when visiting anglers could come for two, three, four weeks at a time, settling into the relaxed rhythm of their days with time on their hands. Modern life has it that we grab snatches of fishing days when we can.

If I could fish each of these places at least once in my lifetime I would be happy and I'm slowly ticking them off my bucket list. This time, as I leave Ballynahinch, I'm back on the N59 to Clifden. I'm going north, having decided to return to Leenane and Delphi where I've some unfinished business.

Earlier in the year when I met Peter Mantle I never got to fish the Delphi fishery and this would be my opportunity to set that right. I want to experience its waters, fishing and atmosphere for myself and see if there's any lingering spirit of Peter's and some of that craic and bonhomie still around the place.

I follow the road once more into Leenane and drive around the fjord before coming to Delphi Lodge, the long Georgian house overlooking Finlough. The fishery office is open, where the manager Michael is organising anglers and guides on their beats throughout the day.

Michael, it turns out, is also a Dub and like myself has been 'culchified' with a relaxed and easygoing way through years of living in the countryside.

When I first moved to south Tipperary, at the age of thirty, my wife gave me one winter on the farm before I'd go 'running back to Dublin'. But in truth, I was always a culchie at heart. From dogs and fishing, the countryside was where my heart always belonged. The peace and solitude I found during summer holidays in Galway in my mother's old family home was heaven for me.

Michael, Delphi's fishery manager, seemed to have similarly embraced the more laid-back mindset and when I had to change dates at the last minute due to a family illness, it was no hassle: 'Sure there was little water here anyway and you're better off coming another time,' was his friendly response.

Trying to find dates in the calendar was what was, unsurprisingly, proving most difficult. Between kids' parties, work, family, training, birthdays and holidays, the number of weekends that were free over the summer was small. Factor in the trips I wanted to make for bass fishing, and the windows I had for salmon fishing over the summer were dwindling more and more.

At the end of every year I look back on my fishing season and write out in my fishing journal the details of trips made, fish caught, tactics and conditions. But many of the observations remain the same, recurring year after year: 'Need to get out more'; 'Sort out work and career'; 'Sort out downtime and stick to it'; 'Fish more, no excuses!'; 'Establish a routine'. The season starts out full of promise and hope with regular trips earlier on but then, once the summer arrives, it seems to taper away just when the business end of the season is really getting going. Work gets especially busy at this time of year but still, I look back in the dark evenings of winter and wonder why the low number of days out fishing, just when it's most attractive. Fishing is a healing exercise for me, a way to escape the stresses of modern work and life but for some reason I sometimes hold myself back, as if not wanting to push myself out the door, preferring instead to stay at home and internalise the storm of feelings that are crashing inside me.

In my defence, I know that when work takes over, my mind is kept elsewhere. I might be in Tipperary but I'm thinking of work in Dublin and the myriad things that need sorting. Each season I kick and berate myself for not getting out on the river more, wondering is self-sabotage a natural part of being human.

One strategy I now have is to book and pay for the fishing trip well in advance. If it's paid for and set in stone, there's less likelihood of backing out or finding excuses not to go. Today I finally walk into Delphi Lodge, just myself and my rod for some fishing.

It's a typical Georgian house with rich, green ivy on its front while inside, old black and white photos of the building and of anglers fishing on the lake from days gone by hang on the walls. I walk down the corridor and can hear the sounds from a busy kitchen behind one door. Opposite is an open door into Michael Wade's fishery office, a small room with shelves of books and filing cabinets of paperwork.

'I've finally arrived,' I say as I mention my name.

'Better late than never,' he laughs with a hint of his Dublin accent still there.

I buy some salmon flies and am handed a map of the river. Today I'd be fishing the Bundorragha ('bottom of the dark valley') River, a mile-long little gem of a river that cuts through the valley, only 20 yards wide, flowing from Finlough in a series of rapids, smaller waterfalls and pools before reaching the sea at Killary Harbour. I'd been told by Michael that, despite the rain, the lakes would help wash out the river and it would settle down quickly. I would be starting at a section of the river half a mile downstream from the lodge that flows into a wide pool at a bend before continuing further on.

The rain had finally eased and the sun was shining high as I drove down to the beat and parked in a lay-by. The road travels alongside the Bundorragha but even though cars pass by you throughout the day, the vast expanse of the landscape that surrounds you swallows you whole. The Mweelrea mountains, a horseshoe-shaped range between Galway and Mayo with the highest peak in Connemara at 814 metres, look down as I cast a line out onto the river.

But my eyes have to focus down, not up, and keeping back from the edge, it's easy casting to the far side of the river. The rocky, rugged landscape means there are little or no trees or bushes to hamper one's casting and only a single-handed rod is needed to get the line out onto the water. The river is starting to come down after the heavy rains but with a strong flow still, and I can see about a foot into the water as I search eagerly for signs of a salmon.

The river is a mix of different pools, seams and currents produced by the rocks and boulders that lie in its path, some

Haunted by Waters

visible above the water but most hidden underneath. Drifts with the fly are short as you search for the pockets of water where the salmon should be. I cast and walk downstream, cast and walk downstream again, coming to a small pool just above a sharp bend. It should be an obvious holding spot for a salmon and just to be careful, I strip off some more line so as to keep my distance.

I watch the line intently as it floats slowly downstream in the smooth waters, unhindered by any cross-currents. A few feet under the surface is my shrimp-style fly, a traditional Irish pattern of feathers and thread in the shape of a shrimp. As salmon don't feed when they return to the river to spawn, the hope for anglers is to show them a fly to resemble something they were used to seeing out in the ocean. They might not be hungry but if you can get a fly to float past them and they are in the mood then you just might annoy them enough to have them snatch at it.

And then my line gets pulled from my hand. I hold my breath and wait. Tug-tug, there it is; tug-tug-tug again. There's no doubt about it. I strike up with my rod and feel the resistance of a fish on the hook. I'm into a salmon and I watch in delight as the fish on the line races off, trying to escape. The battle is a good one as each time I get the salmon closer to the bank it has other ideas and races off into the current.

But finally, with my arms beginning to tire, the fish is also tiring and I see his head coming to the surface. I still have no net on me but find a stony, shallow bank where I'm able to bring the salmon ashore. It's a fine 10 lbs, I estimate as I pull it out of the water, but my heart sinks a little as it's not the pristine, shining silver of a fresh fish that I was hoping for. Instead this salmon is slightly coloured from having been in the river a number of weeks. Salmon lose their silver sheen the longer they spend in fresh water as they make their way upstream to spawn and it is the bright silver ones that are the most prized and admired.

I tell myself off however for harbouring any disappointments – it's a salmon caught and landed on the fly and it's a beautiful creature to admire, fresh or not. I got to feel the heart-stopping take and fight and am holding a respectably sized fish that has travelled thousands of miles across the Atlantic to return to the same river of its birth to spawn and continue the lifecycle of this remarkable species. I've nothing but admiration for this heroic fish and after a quick picture I put him back into the water to swim away and continue on his journey. I've just been a spectator intruding on his life's purpose and for that opportunity I am thankful.

Peter Mantle's words echo in my head as I watch the salmon's shadow disappear into the waters: *'I have always thought salmon fishing is a pretty weird form of madness … we're fishing for a fish that isn't feeding, we have no idea why they take a fly, which the great majority of the time they don't …'*

But still I'm here. If showing up is half the battle, then at least I've given myself a chance. I've pushed myself out the door and am standing on the river's edge. Sometimes it's easier to hold ourselves back and not make the effort, staying behind our front door rather than going out into the world and taking life's ups and downs in our stride as part of the experience.

Before coming to Connemara I was lost in a fog of stress

and self-doubt, weighed down by work. The last thing I felt I could do was drive halfway across the country to spend time fishing. But I did it because I had booked and paid for it weeks in advance – forcing myself into it – and now here I am having caught a salmon in the wilds of the Delphi Valley. I take a deep breath and feel a sense of belonging and calm return once again. It's about salmon fishing and it's about so much more.

8.
Bass Mecca on Cork's Atlantic Coast

*I*t's August and starting to get hot. Not like the drought of 2018, but it's shaping up to be another dry summer.

Meeting two French people in a shop in Clonmel recently, they explained that they had moved here 'because of the people, but also the weather in France is getting crazy, too hot …' When French people are moving to Ireland for a nicer climate, then things must be getting bad.

In the height of the summer when the rivers are low and salmon and brown trout are harder to come by, my favourite place to go to cast a line and feel a bend in the rod is the sea.

Willing to cast a fly or lure at most fish, I was intrigued and drawn in by the possibility of saltwater fishing for bass. I grew up by the sea and for most of my life was within view of it.

Brought up on the northside of Dublin within a short walk of Dollymount Beach and the Bull Island causeway, I went to secondary school in Sutton on the way up to Howth Head and even when my family emigrated to Australia when I was ten, we lived near the sea in a south Sydney suburb.

My mother's family's home in Galway overlooked the bay, while a later family move during my college years to north County Dublin had us literally within a stone's throw of the beach and Lambay Island. College summers spent in America and the UK invariably had me beside the coast, from Jersey Island to the spectacular Cape May on the southern tip of New

Jersey. Even the first property myself and my wife bought in Raheny was a few hundred metres from the coast and when I opened the windows I could hear the seagulls cawing overhead.

The sea was always there, never far away, but I suppose it was something that I took for granted. During my college years, walking home from the train station in Malahide, I appreciated its company as the path ran beside the sea wall, smelling the sea air, hearing the gulls and keeping an eye out on the lapping waters for any signs of fish. Thinking back, it seems strange that growing up, all of my fishing was done inland on canals, rivers or lakes. Sea fishing never came onto my radar.

It's peaceful and beautiful in Tipperary, spacious and solitary, and I wouldn't swap it for the world. Except for the lack of the seagulls calling.

Looming mountain peaks and rolling fields are a much different vista from what I was used to. Looking out from the window across to the Knockmealdowns and the Vee, where the drive up through the mountains brings you into Waterford, I'm always conscious that on the other side is Dungarvan and the coast.

If you climb some of the higher peaks they say you can even see the ocean on a clear day but from my window, looking out from the landlocked side, all I can do is imagine. It's heartening to know it's there, though.

It's probably what led me to first seeking out bass fishing a number of years ago, or maybe it was because I was becoming so obsessed with fly fishing – any fly fishing – that I wanted to also try it in the sea.

'A bass mecca' is how Ireland's southern coastline is often described by visiting European saltwater anglers. The Atlantic coast, from Wexford in the south-east, to Waterford and the Copper Coast, to Cork and its myriad bays, coves and inlets, on to the rich waters of Kerry and even the untapped potential of Limerick and Clare's coastline, the pristine and untouched waters are a bass heaven for its aficionados.

There's a synchronicity to the tides, the moon phases and the ocean that gives it a certain romanticism, I like to think. Rivers and lakes have beginnings and ends, but the sea goes ever on, and standing on the rocks as the waves crash all around you makes you feel that bit smaller in the grand scheme of things.

It can be easy to forget that 70 per cent of the earth is covered by the sea and yet only 20 per cent of it has been mapped. It is still the great unknown, untamed, a mass of body from the calm and serene to the raging and the wild. The sea has a way of reminding us of our insignificance in the world.

I have ventured out with rod in hand and there have been many blank sessions and lost fish between Waterford and Cork, cursing the bass and my basic knowledge and skills. I need to learn more and find out what the sea can teach me. That's why today I'm heading south, driving to west Cork. I want to see the coast again, to hear the Atlantic knocking on the door of the shore, to taste the salt and feel that openness that only comes with standing in the sea and looking out at the distant horizon.

I'm being guided by David Norman, a Clonakilty-based guide and expert. I had met David on a previous trip and was struck by his earnest intelligence and curiosity about the ocean and the fish.

He wasn't in it just for the fishing or catching anymore, he was out night after night, session after session all through the year, on his own or with clients, because he wanted to – needed to – find out as much as he could about the bass. And the more he discovered, the more the fish tantalised and intrigued him with more questions than answers.

David and the many other fishing guides and experts like him, including the ones I meet this year, are similar people. They're chasing the horizon. They know they'll never get there but each time they're out on the water they're learning something new, something that gives them a greater understanding and appreciation of their quarry and places them even deeper into the waters around them. For David and local anglers, just fishing the beaches, coves and inlets a few miles east and west of Clonakilty would be enough for a lifetime of exploration.

'West Cork is just cove after cove every step of the way,' says David. 'It's unlimited potential and the fishing pressure isn't as much in this part of Ireland. I have had people visiting and the reason they came is because it's a little bit under the radar. The difference is, if you go into Wexford, if you talk to people and you say you're going fishing, they say "bass", whereas here in west Cork it's not so well known. I would say that while the fishing isn't as strong as Kerry, Waterford or Wexford, I think as a destination it can be pretty damn good.'

He's right, there is something special about west Cork, and not just in terms of fishing. The first time I was in Clonakilty I visited a small local bar in the afternoon. Lunch was over and I wondered if I might be able to get a sandwich or a snack. Ten minutes later, the barman came down the spiral staircase carrying a wooden board of cheeses, cold meats, chutney and fruit.

'I was only expecting a ham and cheese sandwich,' I told him in surprise.

'Sure that's how we do it in Clon!' he replied with a beaming smile.

Go west past Kinsale along the coast and there's a special vibe to the place. Maybe it's the sea, the coves, beaches and the bays with the roads circling around the headlands right next to them; maybe it's the food, the people, the atmosphere, but all I know is every summer I have to get back to west Cork with my family to experience it all again. The fishing too has become an increasingly important part of that.

It was the special atmosphere of the area that also lured David Norman here in the first place, though it was an Irish woman who brought him over. He's British navy by background but after five years he returned to civilian life, albeit with the call of the sea always haunting him. Growing up in the south-east of England, he says, he always had the sea around him. When he went into the workforce after the navy, his main passion was windsurfing and that kept him connected to the sea.

Meeting a Galway woman in Ireland at one of the competitions saw him flying back to Ireland whenever he could until he finally decided to move over full-time from England.

'The south-east of England is the total opposite to here in terms of the pressures and quality of life,' he explains. 'I thought, well, I love Ireland and at least if I go over it gives me a chance. I was actually able to transfer over with my company to Cork.

'I looked south and I saw Kinsale. Then I looked along the coast and I saw this Clonakilty place and I asked my now-wife, "What's this place like?"

"I don't know, it's kind of known for music," she told me. I definitely wanted to live on the coast because I was keen on windsurfing and so we drove here one summer's evening, the sun was shining, we had a great meal, we looked around and I said, "This has got to be the spot."'

He was a windsurfer then but as the body gets older, the aches and pains of the sport take longer to recover from until eventually in your thirties (or whenever your body tells you) you realise you can't keep doing it.

He had to keep in touch with the ocean though, no matter what, and he fell into bass fishing as a natural extension of his love of the sea and being outdoors. He hadn't fished for years, although he grew up catching minnows and whatever else came along the shore near to where he lived.

The navy and then work life put a halt to any more fishing dreams, but settling down to life in west Cork and with windsurfing having to take a back seat, he once more found himself picking up a rod. There were miles and miles of beaches, coves, inlets and strands to be explored, all within a short drive of where he lived, and he set out to find out as much as he could.

'I was looking for something to do and to fill some time,' he remembers. 'I'm quite obsessive. I wanted to get further and deeper into it. But it was also about making me feel alive.'

As the weeks turned into months, he still wasn't able to catch a bass. They just weren't cooperating and he wasn't tuned into their idiosyncrasies. Tides, weather, moon, waves – they were always changing, and the bass reacted differently each time. It was about just putting in the time, though. Most people would have given up. David Norman wasn't most people.

First of all, he says, he just loved being out on the coast. There were even cross-overs to his windsurfing days because you're constantly moving around, finding the conditions that are optimal.

Slowly but surely, he was starting to find his feet – as well as the fish. The bass started to be caught; not just in good conditions but when it was fizzing up, weedy, blowing a gale and downright nasty, all through the year.

Now you start to get a picture of the bass-angler-as-obsessive. That, and the attention to detail and being used to spending hours on your own. Well, not on your own, exactly. It's you and the ocean, after all, trying to crack the code of the conditions at a particular moment in time to outwit the sea's silver hunters.

He first started guiding when his father-in-law, a keen salmon angler, came to visit. No pressure, then. They were to go to a regular mark he knew well at low tide at 5 p.m. Just to be on the safe side, David decided to fish it twelve hours earlier to see what was going on.

'There was something going on,' he recalls. 'It was just an incredible event: there were bass everywhere. I didn't tell my father-in-law that, of course, and come 5 p.m. I walked him down the beach and I hooked a fish before he'd even put his line through the rings of his rod. Sure enough, soon afterwards he caught his first bass and it just went on from there.'

Helping people to catch fish gives him even more of a thrill these days but he remains careful – and wary – of giving away the marks in pictures on social media. He's even had people friending him on these platforms trying to worm their way into his trust, to prise from him the information he has built up over years of practice and hard yards.

'A lot of people who contact me to guide them, I won't even take them out,' he admits. 'I have a quick look at their profile on Facebook and I can see that no, we're not like-minded people so we won't be fishing together. It's not just people taking fish, it's angling pressure as well, if too many people turn up on that spot the fish just won't be there.'

West Cork is still a bit under the radar, he believes, and he hopes it stays that way. Instead, it's probably more the surf culture that dominates around Clonakilty.

'I think of this place as a destination. It may not be the most hard-core fishing but it can be pretty damn good. Now, if you take the Copper Coast from Tramore to Dungarvan [the 17-km stretch of Waterford coastline so-called because of the copper mines that existed there in the nineteenth century and an under-explored coast of cliffs, rock formations and beaches] there's almost too much good ground. It's as if God had designed the best bass coastline, and there's actually probably too much for an angler because it's almost impossible to be in the right place; you've got to cover a lot of ground too. It pays to really focus on a small area rather than spread yourself too thin.'

David has fished all of the best bass spots all over the country, from Galway around to Wexford, from spring right through to winter, but it all still leads him back to the local and what he knows best.

You can't go far in west Cork either without hearing an English or European accent; they're either tourists passing through for the summer or have, like David, decided to move over altogether. Invariably, many of them are here for the lifestyle and the outdoors such as the fishing or surfing.

'I'm sure everyone's got a different story,' David says. 'But I do know that in the UK everyone would love to move to Devon or Cornwall, but the difference between Devon, Cornwall and here is it's massively over-populated over there. All the towns are kind of built out and the roads are extremely small. I think we've got what Devon and Cornwall have but we also still have a very low population.'

Times are changing, though. Populations are expanding, towns and beaches are getting busier, but thankfully the Irish spirit and culture is still holding on. What is struggling, however, is the fishing. Like other areas of angling, bass fishing has become more difficult and the catches aren't what they used to be from even just a few years ago. How common a refrain has that become in all areas of fishing.

'One train of thought is that the fish are getting wiser and I've always thought, as catch-and-release anglers are we basically giving this whole educational programme to bass? If every competent bass angler catches fifty or one hundred bass each year and then we're releasing 99 per cent of those fish? I mean over time it would make sense that they're kind of wising up a bit.'

Bass and mullet also need more protection. Bass are extremely slow-growing, so a 10-lb bass could be twenty years old. Inland Fisheries Ireland is doing tagging, scale sampling and logbooks to know more and there's been an interesting study in Cork Harbour that showed that bass are very similar to salmon in that they return to the same estuary system. It's something that David has seen with his own eyes in west Cork.

'There's one particular bass that I'd been watching for about eight weeks. Every day he came back to the same spot and just sat there in the estuary waiting for the tide to flood. That's what makes them vulnerable, returning to the same spots time and time again.'

David has had to experiment and change tactics, seeing what worked when the usual tried and tested methods were not getting the results.

'As the day fishing tapered off, I found the night fishing picked up and now *that's* tapering off so what's next I don't know … I don't want to think about it. "Why?" is the million-dollar question. But it has got consistently harder and harder. You just need settled conditions and the reality is conditions are becoming less settled. The marine environment is under huge pressure.'

Change. That is the word on every angler's lips, and anyone working in or around the environment – in fact, anyone with an interest in the outside world – can't help but notice it. The climate is changing, weather patterns are becoming more extreme and unpredictable and the oceans are heating up.

While a lot of focus in recent years has been on the impact of carbon emissions on the atmosphere, it is the oceans that absorb 93 per cent of the extra energy from the greenhouse gas effect. They are warming up and becoming more acidic, killing off plant life and species, and we still don't know the true effect this is having on the feeding and spawning grounds in the deep oceanic waters.

Guides and anglers like David have to adapt and he finds himself either going further out to sea in a kayak to find the fish, or else having to fish at night from the shore.

'Even though I was becoming more knowledgeable,' he explains, 'with better equipped state-of-the-art equipment, really tuning in to the conditions, having every opportunity to go, and yet the results were just going down and down. Then, about five years ago, a very good friend of mine here locally was fishing at night – really just out of necessity because he had a young family – and I'll never forget one particular summer's evening I fished from 8 p.m. until 10 p.m. and caught nothing. He fished from 10 p.m. until midnight and caught fish – three to four fish – and he was doing that consistently.

'It was obviously telling me something. That the fish were more confident to feed after dark and that's the way it's just kind of gone. Having said that, the night fishing results are definitely going backwards as well. I do what I do results-wise, but I'd still rather be out in the daylight enjoying everything that's going on around me. Though there is a certain thrill in night fishing. It is very special to be out at night. Some of the things that you see and you experience are just different. When it's quiet and you're slowly retrieving a lure or fly through the water and all of a sudden it gets hit ... your senses just go through the roof ... this takes you to a whole new level.'

Fly fishing is still David's preferred way to catch bass, but sometimes beggars can't be choosers.

Every autumn he makes the trip to Cape Cod to fish their bass striper run. At least when he's fishing over there he knows he's going to be catching – it's not a case of if, but how many and how big. Fly fishing for bass on this side of the Atlantic is anything but as clear-cut. The challenge to catch bass on the fly is huge and there are times when needs must.

'It's more a choice between some fish and no fish and even with really good fly anglers they'll tell you there's a lot of times it's no fish. For the effort I'm putting in, I still want a reasonable return. I do see more fly fishing in my future but it's hard to justify it. I'm better off finding them on the lure first.'

If Ireland is considered a 'promised land' for bass angling, it's our visiting British and European anglers who are teaching us and showing us how to be better anglers. They are bringing new techniques, new styles, new set-ups and approaches that are educating us and opening our eyes to what can be achieved with a bit more outside-the-box thinking. For David, it was the French, American and Japanese bass anglers whom he learned the most from.

'It was very primitive here, but it's gone particularly high-tech now,' says David. 'It has been about adopting techniques from Japan and from the United States where they fish for large and small freshwater bass and the striper. We've got the very latest carbon fibre rods from Japan, the very latest braids – the technology we have at our disposal is just world-class. The problem is, the better equipped we get and the more

Haunted by Waters

knowledgeable we become, the more the results seem to be going backwards.

'The only good thing is, though, the harder it gets, the less people will do it, which will take the pressure off. In the last month I think I saw two other anglers in the distance and that was only because I had binoculars! The average person is just able to head out on a Sunday afternoon whereas I'll plan my fishing for weeks in advance going in the early hours of Tuesday morning or something like that, because that's when it's the right time and it lines up with the weather, tides and conditions.'

I am one of those Sunday afternoon anglers, and being a fly angler of multiple interests – salmon, trout, bass, pike – I find it hard even narrowing down and focusing my choice; sometimes too much choice can be a bad thing. I've found I needed to be more disciplined in my approach, focusing on brown trout in the key moments around duck fly or mayfly time, bass in the summer and into the autumn around key tides, pike in the autumn and winter, and salmon throughout the year when time and water height allowed.

Before becoming a full-time guide, David worked for the same company for twenty-seven years and I have friends who have stayed in the same job all of their lives. But it's not something that I could ever have envisaged myself doing. Often I wonder if I'd be better off being an angler like David, concentrating on the one species of fish – even just the one way of catching them – and increasing my success rate in the process. That's not me, though, not as an angler, nor as a person. I've often thought it's to the detriment of a lot of my career, seeking interests from a wide array of places, never staying in one place or happy with my lot. Even when I played sport growing up, there was soccer, Gaelic football, basketball, hockey, tennis, badminton. Jack of all trades and master of none seems to have been my path. 'Find your one thing, your one over-riding passion,' the life coaches of this world say, but what if there is no one single thing, I ask myself, what if one's interests are sparked by the potential of multiple areas to explore?

While David has his sights constantly on bass fishing, I can see the waves on a summer's day and think 'bass', but I also see rain after a dry spell and think 'salmon'; I see the midges out and about and I think 'trout rising'; and I see frost on the ground and think 'time for pike'.

Most of the guides you meet in this book have all chosen one type of fish and fishing to dedicate themselves to. Or maybe it chose them, but either way, they couldn't let it go, this was what they were always going to do. I envy those people. It's in complete contrast to my own restlessness, my need to move on and try other things. Maybe, though, fishing is my way of stopping, my chance to slow down.

For tonight, for a few hours at least, I'd be in the hands of one of those experts as we pursued bass in the night-time surf. We were heading to a few different marks and we would start targeting these areas just at the turn of the ebbing tide.

It was no surprise when David told me he'd already been out in the same places at the same time days earlier, just to be sure, and yes, there were bass about. 'There are fish there,' he says confidently.

The appetite and expectations were suitably whetted. I had never fished in the surf at night before and while I was excited at what it might bring, part of me was still nervous, apprehensive. Standing in the ocean in the dark with crashing waves up to your waist can be physically and mentally enduring. Safety would be paramount. I looked out at the ocean and knew that my excitement was going to outweigh any concerns or nerves. The sea was out there. I wanted to experience everything it had.

Night fishing for bass was going to be a new experience for me and an exciting one. There was a new moon in the sky which would give us better cover and by 9.30 p.m. David and I were tackled up and ready, setting out along the beach heading into the night, the surf full of hope and expectation.

'You know, despite all the difficulties being experienced in bass fishing,' David tells me, unprompted, 'I still love my fishing. Let's face it, if it was easy, we wouldn't be doing it, would we? You can only work with what's there but my fishing is a constant evolution, I'm constantly moving forward in some direction. Look at how many other things you could be doing instead.'

We walk out and the first wave comes crashing against my waders. It feels cold and slightly unnerving. I cast out into the gloaming evening, the surf all around me and the bass out there somewhere.

Casting into the dark is something else. There's nothing quite like it and it's hard to truly describe it. At our first mark we waded thigh-deep into the oncoming surf. The waves arrive in front of us ready to hit land and we are their barrier. Most of the waves hit and fall around you but occasionally one takes you unawares and smacks you hard on its arrival, unexpected. On these occasions it feels like you're in the boxing ring and have got caught with a sucker punch in your midriff.

David looks back and sees I'm still standing, still casting. All is okay then and he turns back to the water, scanning the waves in front of us, working out the puzzle in his head, trying to find the fish. I can sense that *Where are the bass?* is constantly whirring in his mind as we prowl along the coast.

The pitch blackness is offset by the constant thundering swell rocking in towards us, crashing in front, around and behind us and I'm seeing the landscape from another perspective altogether. House lights are dotted around the coastline, while the rotating beam of a far-off lighthouse acts as the anchor to guide us along this stretch of beach.

What's most beautiful however is what is above us, where a blanket of stars is laid out in the night sky, the likes of which I have rarely experienced before. I'm realising how little we need daylight to appreciate what is around us; night-time can teach us so much more.

In the darkness you only have yourself and your breathing – attention slows down and you are forced to take it all in. It's moments like these that I've been searching for, that sense of stepping back and regaining something that's been lost in the predictability of life.

And when I look down, the scene just takes my breath away. It's as if the stars have fallen to the water and are shimmering around my feet just for me. It is the sand eels, electric in the night light, darting all around us, their reflections shimmering in the water.

But I don't see sand eels, I just see the magic and believe they are the stars in the sky come down for me. As I stand staring in awe, David has inched closer and says quietly, 'Now look at the waves in front and tell me if you can see anything in them.'

I raise my eyes from the shimmering starlights in the water to the waves building to a crescendo thirty yards in front of us. But it's not just the waves or the usual white horses that I see; instead, there's a blue tinge to the whole scene playing out. I scan across the breaking wave line to double check, and yes, there is an unrecognisable blue hue dancing around the white-water foam like a laser light show has just been switched on.

'But how?' I ask out loud.

'It's bioluminescence from organisms in the sea,' David explains. 'That's what's causing the effect.'

'Ireland's own Aurora Borealis,' I say breathlessly.

'Right, now back to the fishing.' David awakens me from my awed reverie and it's back to the job at hand. We're still here to catch some bass, after all. I cast out again into the surf. This time the blue glow has disappeared and I half wonder if I imagined it all.

We're nearly an hour into the fishing now and the night has settled in. There's been the occasional tap on the line but nothing solid. My eyes have become used to the darkness and my body is getting accustomed to the rhythm of the waves crashing into me. The temperature has dropped and there's a chill to the air. I tighten my fishing jacket even more.

'They're there, they're there,' David reassures me as we cast and walk down the shore. 'The taps could be small schoolies, even sea trout. If we don't have any action in the next few minutes we can look at changing it up.'

Those next few minutes never came. Very soon after, I cast out into the pounding surf, not doing anything different when – *clunk* – the line stopped, and the rod tip began to bend. I didn't want to strike too early but then again I didn't want to lose this first (and only?) chance of a bass tonight.

I held my breath and let the tip bend again – *clunk* – it went down once more and this time even more firmly. With conviction, I struck the rod up and I was in – I could feel the bass at the end of my line.

'Fish on!' I shout, trying to appear calm but in truth my heart is racing fast as I fight the bass that is trying to escape into the surf. David runs over to help.

'Okay, quickly now, start walking back to shore. Quickly now, quickly!'

He didn't want me to lose this fish either.

I take a few steps but then have to let the fish run as it fights back, using the strength of the waves and the tide to resist. But the hook holds firm. Though I'm not sure the same could be said for myself. I nearly stumble in the water as I back up to the shore, my focus always on the rod tip and keeping tension on the line. The runs keep going and I hold firm, watching the rod bend into the butt, hoping and praying it will all hold up.

Gradually the runs become shorter and less explosive. The shoreline was close to hand, if I could get it to land then it would be mine. In the shallower water I can feel the weight of the fish increase on my line. It's a decent fish, I think. Not a schoolie, but a decent fish.

'Keep going,' David instructs me as I reach the beach. He grabs the leader and then tries to grab the bass by its mouth. For an instant I thought my worst nightmare would come true as I see him reach down and then suddenly lunge into the shallow water. After all the effort, has the fish escaped at the last minute?

But David stands up, beaming, holding my bass. Not just any bass. An absolute lunker, the biggest I had ever seen this close. Its length, its depth were a sight to behold, much bigger than the usual schoolie-sized bass I had caught before.

'Bloody hell! What a fish! I can't believe it!' I say over and over. Words are coming out of me like gibberish as I just stand there staring and pointing at this monster bass that David holds in front of me. He hands the fish over, my fingers wrapping around its hard bottom lip and its weight sags on my arm as I hold it for some quick photos.

'The weight of it!' I exclaim, having trouble keeping it upright and off the ground.

'Definitely bigger than I expected,' nods David, just as happy.

On the sand, I proudly hold the bass aloft. My biggest bass to date and in the pitch black of the night. The waves still crashed behind me and how many other wonders, I could only guess.

We didn't have a scales with us but David had a tape measure and measured from the mouth to the tail of the fish.

'You won't believe this, but it's a 75-cm bass. That's 8½ lbs, the biggest fish I know of that's been caught this season!' he tells me in delight.

These weren't words I was used to hearing when it came to my fishing and I was speechless, taking in this amazing creature before me: a hefty 8½ lbs of silver-grey with its spiny fins, the power in its flank and tail to live out its long life in the waters of the Atlantic Ocean. An incredible fish.

'Thank you,' was all I could manage, and it wasn't clear if it was to David or the fish I was talking, but it was time to put it back. We found the shallows, a quieter spot away from the main surf, and I got down on my knees in the water to hold this silver beauty of the sea one last time.

After a few minutes she was ready to swim away and I watched her strong tail swimming back out to the open sea. Would I ever experience a bass as big as this again in my lifetime? This was a personal best to beat a personal best and I stood staring out to sea. Was this as good as it got? I wanted to savour it, remember it, store it away and be telling my children and grandchildren about the day I caught my biggest bass.

'Come on, let's go back to the rocks and tackle up again,' said David impatiently. 'I reckon you'll need a few minutes to come down from that rush before you can start fishing again.'

He was right; I did need to come down from my high and get my heart back to its normal pace. I sat on the rocks in the glow of David's headlamp while he rigged the rod up again, checking the knots, hook and line.

'Ready?' he said after a few minutes.

'Absolutely,' I say, grinning from ear to ear.

We caught more bass that night from a few more marks but nothing was to compare to that first fish. At one point during the fishing, the oily blackness of the ocean merged with the night sky and for a few moments as I stood there in the surf I couldn't tell where sea or sky began and ended. Dazed and confused by it all, it felt like I was standing in a Turner painting, experiencing the chaos, confusion and deepness of it all. Then the moment passed, waves washed in, clouds passed by and I was set right, back in the presence of my place in the world again.

It was 3 a.m. by the time we finally made our way out of the sea and headed back to the cars. We were weary but happy anglers as we changed out of our sea-soaked waders. The cold of the night was starting to seep in, I was shivering and I was keen to get into my warm car and hit the road.

David was right, though: everything had aligned and it was a night to remember.

'Let me know when we can do it again,' I told him as we parted. 'More of that, please.'

He laughed and said he'd see what he could do.

I drove home, the roads eerily quiet, apart from the odd taxi driver or garda car. I was leaving west Cork behind me heading back to Tipp and my family. It would be nearly 5 a.m. by the time I tip-toed back into the house, the sun beginning to rise, my wife and the kids all asleep and the dogs snoring in their beds.

I took off my shoes and dropped onto the couch, not daring to risk climbing the stairs and waking the family. Pulling a blanket over me I curled into the darkest corner to keep out the growing light. I would be woken in two hours by the kids and their usual morning routine, but it didn't matter.

Wait till I'd told them all about my adventures in the sea at night and the story of the giant bass I'd caught and landed. I would tell them of the magical blue lights in the waves and the shimmering stars fallen into the water that danced all around me.

I fell into a deep sleep dreaming of it all. That night I felt like one of the Darling children befriended by Peter Pan. The magic of fishing come true. Come Monday the grind of work would begin again but it would be different: *I* would be different. The moments and memories of the night's fishing would stay with me for a long time, a salve to return to when working on late-night deadlines, my own mindfulness to take with me for the start of the working week.

9.

The Dodder and Dublin's City Depths

T

he seagulls could be heard in the city, squawking overhead. The call of the sea is never too far, even in the busy heart of Dublin, Ireland's capital city. Walking through the financial services district, the Luas trundles by, buses and cars zoom past and the DART rumbles across the bridge. This is the city, but forever echoing in its midst are the gulls. Hovering, diving, skirting, being blown by the wind over multi-storey office blocks.

I cross the River Liffey, reminded of the waters that are never far from our urban hearts; cities and towns built around the commerce, food and transport that rivers could bring. Now, thousands of us cross the same waters every day without a moment's thought to look down. The river is dark and stagnant, appearing lifeless to the bustling life of the city towering above.

But stop and look closer. Flowing under the steel arches, hiding out of sight, skitting past human eyes are the fish still living below the depths, largely ignored. Still existing, still making their darting ways through waves, the murk and the undergrowth, navigating shopping trolleys, human rubbish and waste, and somehow surviving.

It's a remarkable fact that salmon are still making their way from the feeding grounds of the Atlantic, circumnavigating the Irish coastline and finding their way up to Dublin Bay. From there they manage to make it through the waters and the city, waiting for high tide to help push them through, pausing only briefly as they swim upstream of the Liffey and on through the city.

From surviving the wild rigours of the Atlantic Ocean, this last stretch is a much shorter, but no less hazardous few miles back up to the higher waters where they were born. Some salmon make it to the quieter surroundings and slower glides beyond to the Strawberry Beds, Islandbridge and Leixlip, environments more akin to salmon fishing. Leixlip, after all, comes from the old Norse *Lax-hlaup* meaning 'salmon leap'. The name in Irish, *Léim an Bhradáin*, is a direct translation of this, while in Latin, it is *Saltus salmonis*.

The Liffey used to regularly have the first salmon of the year caught in Ireland, and while fish numbers and anglers have declined in recent times, hardy souls still venture out on frosty New Year's Day mornings to cast a line more in tradition than hope. It's not confined to 1 January though – salmon anglers catch fish throughout the year, with grilse caught during the summer runs and fish leaping the weirs in Lucan and Leixlip still a sight to behold.

Other fish veer off before Islandbridge and the upper reaches of the Liffey, instead finding their way up feeder rivers and it is to one of these that I make my way to fish and find out more about the fly fishing opportunities available in the depths of the city.

When I'm working in Dublin during the week my heart aches for the quiet countryside, but I have been reading about the brown trout and sea trout that can be caught on the River Dodder which flows through the south of Dublin. This Monday in September as I travel to Dublin for work meetings, I pack not only my laptop but a rod, my wellingtons and a box of flies. I board the early-morning train bound for Heuston, packed with other workers, and set my rod tube beside my bag. Somehow, just seeing the rod gives me a sense of calm, as if I'm not leaving the countryside entirely behind me. I take my laptop out. I still have a day's work ahead of me before I visit the Dodder later on but I can feel more settled already, the tensions of the day ahead beginning to evaporate. It's been nine months since I began my conscious journey of regular fishing trips and I can feel its effects on me. The trips booked in advance have given me something to look forward to, counting down the days to my escape to the different places and waters. It's about the journey and not the destination, it's said, and as I take my seat on this morning's train journey, I know I have something more to look forward to this day.

The River Dodder makes its way from the Wicklow mountains to the south of Dublin through the suburbs before finally joining the Liffey just before the sea at Ringsend. As with most rivers, it takes a meandering course, as if trying to find its way in the dark before emerging into the sunlight and the great expanse of water waiting for it. Remarkably, for a river that has seen so much housing and urbanisation built up around it, the Dodder has survived. It's been culverted (channelled) in places, especially when meeting industrial estates and roads, but it still comes out on the other side, stubbornly determined to see its way through.

And the same can be said for the fish. In the lower reaches especially, as the river flows through leafier suburbs and parks, free rising brown trout have been a common sight throughout the Dodder's life. Thanks to concerted efforts from organisations such as the Dodder Anglers' Association, Inland Fisheries Ireland, Dodder Action Group, local volunteers and keen-eyed observers and guardians of the waters, battles against pollution, developers and waste have been constantly waged. Never letting up, these battles have been increasingly won.

I have passed through these suburbs innumerable times, on a bus, in a car or walking. I've been in Donnybrook crossing over the bridge, the bus station on one side and the Dodder River, incongruous almost against its urban surroundings, on the other. How many cars pass over the bridge's spans on a daily basis, making their way into the city in the morning and back out in the evening oblivious to what lies below, I wonder.

The Dodder has been enjoying something of a resurgence in recent years. Despite all the building development – the new houses, offices and industrial estates – somehow the river has held on and the fish in it have thrived, even withstanding pollution and fish-kills, with the Dodder Anglers' Association to the forefront of its salvation.

The club was formed in the late 1950s following a severe fish kill, with the aim of protecting the river and its inhabitants, but a second major incident occurred in 1975 when effluent from an illegal industrial dump wiped out the fish stock downstream as far as the sea.

If it wasn't for the early efforts of pioneers such as Ned Cusack, who had become involved because of the initial pollution in the 1950s, and who recognised the need to blood the next generation in the appreciation and care of the river, who knows what would

Haunted by Waters

be flowing through the south Dublin suburbs today? The Dodder Anglers' Association now boasts over a thousand members and is one of the biggest angling clubs in Europe.

Cusack was in his thirties when he started to introduce young local kids to the joys of the Dodder and all that it contained. The youngsters were enthralled with learning how to tie flies, watching fishing films in the winter and identifying the different flies and how to match the hatch in the spring and summer time. Ken Whelan and his brother were two impressionable young boys who were in thrall to the magic of fishing and the river. Ken is now an internationally renowned fisheries scientist, travelling the world advising on fish habitats and conservation, but growing up in south Dublin it was people like Ned Cusack who opened his eyes to what the Dodder could offer.

Ken is also an avid fly angler and author of *Nomad of the Tides*, a seminal work on Irish sea trout fishing, and before I travel to Dublin I reach out to him to see if he can show me the fishing in the city. He agrees enthusiastically and the evening can't come fast enough. Meetings seem to drone on interminably during the day and I catch myself checking the time on my phone for the umpteenth time. I get some strange looks as I lug my rod tube around with me but when I start to explain about the Dodder and its salmon and sea trout, I can see my colleagues' eyes begin to glaze over. I'm talking a different language here in the city.

Finally three o'clock comes and I pack away my laptop, jumping on the busy Luas. Before meeting Ken for some evening sea trout fishing, I was determined to experience the daytime brown trout fishing as well. If I could catch one on a dry fly as a double decker bus passed by on a bridge overhead, all the better, but to be casting – and even catching – on the Dodder would be a lifetime's experience fulfilled.

Des Chew of Inland Fisheries Ireland and an expert on the Dodder waters agreed to meet with me and give me some guidance and pointers. Similar to Ken Whelan, his days growing up in Dublin were spent beside the Dodder, fishing it whenever he could.

All of his friends had a rod in their hands at one time or another but as time passed by and they all got older and moved on, only one was still fishing. Des knew then that he wanted to spend his days around the water and the environment and his role as a fisheries protection officer enabled him to do just that.

He was also involved for twelve years with the Dublin Angling Initiative which was set up in 1995 to focus on introducing schoolkids to fishing and nature – be it sea, coarse or game. Over a quarter of a century and 15,000 kids later, it is still going strong, showing kids, mainly from underprivileged backgrounds, the wonders of the water near them.

'The kids might not necessarily live beside a river but they're probably within spitting distance of a river in Dublin that they could fish, so it's about making them aware of the habitat and what they can get from it,' Des tells me as we chat and tackle up by the water's edge near the Dropping Well pub in Milltown.

'The Initiative tries to teach the youngsters how to fish somewhere that's on a public transport route from where they live, so often they're taken fishing to Greystones beach which is on the DART line and they can learn about sea fishing, the coast and how the tide works.

'Then of course we're here on the banks of the lovely River Dodder which has been a teaching ground for many, many youngsters and they can even learn to go on to develop the art of fly fishing here. What gives me the greatest thrill is when I meet the kids years later as grown adults on the rivers fishing and they're teaching *me* a thing or two about it.'

The Dropping Well pub lies beside the banks of the river and the place is beginning to get busy with after-work drinkers, but only a stone's throw away and the river is quiet; just a few dog walkers out alongside us. The only immediate sound is that of water running over the weir, while in the background, the gentle buzz of city traffic passing by.

As I cast out with an 8-foot 4-weight rod and an olive dry fly on the leader, the 142 bus stops behind us, letting out and picking up passengers on its two-mile journey to the city. That's the kind of setting we're in.

And yet, as I turn my back on the road and the traffic and concentrate on my leader, the running water, the heron further downstream and the willows and the ash on the far bank take me far beyond the city and the urban feeling.

'I think I could be on a stream in Connemara,' I tell Des.

'You're right,' he says. 'It's a little piece of heaven and it's on the doorstep for so many. Who says you have to travel across Ireland or the world for wild brown trout fishing? Sometimes I'm actually standing in the river and I'm completely engrossed in what I'm doing, watching my flies go around and then I see a bus go by and I wonder do the people on the bus think I'm mad or are *they* mad for not knowing what's down here?'

It was a few days after a recent flood so the river was coming down nicely and in good order for the fly. Where we stood there were a few beautiful pools and some small weirs with tumbling water.

Olives start flying past us and then I see a fish rising, followed by another, and another. I roll cast to the far bank, aiming for the deeper pools to see if I can tempt one of the risers. The clarity of the water is stunning, something the wildlife, fly hatches and birds attest to as well.

Maybe I'm too busy talking to Des, who stands by my shoulder guiding me, or maybe I'm rusty or taking in everything except my fly because I miss two takes, striking too late. They weren't solid takes, more gentle plucks, but they were still chances gone awry.

'I think it was Peter O'Reilly, the famous game angling author, who once said that if you can catch trout on the Dodder on the dry fly then you can catch fish anywhere,' Des reassures me. 'They're very picky and they can be very cautious about taking the dry fly here.'

I concentrate a bit harder the next few casts. Despite the rises around me, my offering was ignored and so we moved on, down to a riffle of fast, foamy water, switching to tungsten nymphs and searching the river.

Casting out and across, I followed my leader intently. I was determined to land a trout here in the urban wild. Something to cross off that bucket list. Des's words rippled behind me as I cast upstream again. 'That's it, just there, there has to be a fish there now ...'

The line dipped under in a purposeful and oh-so-quick way that it could only be a trout nipping at the fly. I strike downstream and the line tightens. I'm in. The fight is a quick one, with a ½-lb fish coming easily to the net, its striking colours of brown and red spots standing out like panned gold in the daytime sun. I feel like a prospector and while I may not have hit pay dirt, this is a welcome catch any place, any time. As I wet my hands to release the fish, a dog walker continues on behind us as does another bus and the constant stream of traffic.

Fishing on the River Dodder is a remarkable experience. From wild brown trout rising, to elusive salmon and sea trout swimming under the beating heart of the city, it is a unique fly fishing experience as all of urban life passes on by, oblivious to it all.

We continue like this for another hour, meeting fish in the riffles, weirs and faster waters, all the while still seeing them rise on the slower glides. The Dodder has a remarkable variety of water to keep you engaged and entertained. Between nymphs, wets and dries, you'll be kept busy over the course of a few hours, and even then, you've still only travelled a half a mile or so.

There can be building sites on the far bank as you cast or, in one spot in particular, there can be a rhino. I do a double take and turn to Des for an answer as to why a life-sized concrete rhino is suddenly in the middle of the river staring back at us upstream.

'It actually just appeared here one night very mysteriously and it's become a permanent feature along the river, but nobody knows where it came from or how it got there,' Des tries to explain. 'It just arrived and it's stayed ever since, even surviving all the Dodder floods. It's just the kind of stuff you see on the Dodder while fishing for wild brown trout!'

Slightly unnerved, I cast under the intent gaze of an African rhino in the Dublin suburbs. Des is right, where else would you get it? There's something unique and special about this type of fishing and even calling it urban fishing does it a disservice. It's not rough and ready, graffiti-strewn wasteland, it's a free-flowing river in its full health with fish rising and feeding throughout the season.

From Connemara to Dublin, in the blink of an eye and with a rod in the boot of the car or in your work backpack, you could be fishing in your lunchtime for an hour, catching a few trout on the fly before returning to the mundane world of office work. Not a bad way to spend your lunch break.

After a fabulous few hours fishing, dusk was starting to draw in. I say my goodbyes and thanks to Des and I head downstream to meet Ken Whelan, who assured me that in the dark of night we would have a good chance of catching sea trout coming in fresh off the tide.

Ken is softly spoken but his keen, scientific mind lights up when talking about fishing, especially fly fishing. He explained the influence of Ned Cusack, who gave classes to kids like him on the river's wildlife and water cycle.

'Ned Cusack's class was the most incredibly sophisticated biology class you could imagine and all of this was done on a voluntary basis,' Ken recalls of those lucky childhood days. 'We were absolutely captivated by the river, by the flowing water, by the life that was in the river and it became a lot more than angling very quickly. It was our mission to make sure that the river wasn't damaged. We didn't realise it, but by the late 1960s, the fire that was in our bellies was to become so important.'

The suburbs of Dublin expanded rapidly west and south in the 1970s and it was inevitable that rivers like the Dodder would begin to suffer. The answer to sewage from the new housing estates in Tallaght and Templeogue was to get rid of it straight into the river and Ken remembers a pipe that pumped day and night into the Dodder.

They were told it would be sorted, that a scheme would be put in place, and as the problem got worse, it energised people like Ken and Ned Cusack more and more and the numbers joining the angling club increased.

Ned was an army man and a person of principle, and he wasn't afraid to stand up and fight for those principles. By mustering a few hundred people in the angling club, they became an important vote-getter for local politicians.

'Ned realised that by going out and convincing the local communities that something needed to be done, he could actually put together a lobby group that no politician could possibly stand up against,' says Ken.

Ned was instrumental in the formation of the Dodder Valley Association which had nothing to do with angling; it was to do with local people, people who walked their dogs and people who enjoyed being out in the parks beside the river on a summer's evening. It was about giving urban people a little piece of the countryside in their lives.

It was a constant battle however and they couldn't rest on

their laurels. Despite some victories, there was another major pollution incident in 1975. Driven by his lifelong interest in rivers and fish, Ken had qualified as a biologist when he got a phone call one morning to say the fish in the river were all dead. He quickly went into his college to collect bottles for samples and as he approached the river it wasn't just the sight of the dead fish that hit him, it was the smell that was burning his nostrils. This was a chemical dump that would have profound consequences.

Tricresyl phosphate was the guilty substance, an organophosphate compound that is highly toxic and virtually insoluble in water. It had been put into drums and illegally dumped beside the river and when the drums burst, it killed everything along the entire length of its discharge.

Ken quickly began collecting samples, knowing that in addition to the local fisheries board, the association would have to take their own action. His samples were sent to Limerick for testing which revealed the presence of the deadly chemical substance and they began a case against the guilty party which resulted in threats against Ken and others.

'You have to remember,' Ken emphasises, 'there was a lot of distrust towards us at the time. We were seen as being anti-progress and making a fuss over these great new developments. People weren't out there trying to support you – there was no green movement.'

After the economic destitution of the 1940s and '50s, under the Whitaker Plan Ireland in the 1960s and '70s was finally starting to get a glimpse of industrialisation and development. And in the middle were these brave anglers trying, not to stop progress, but to open people's eyes to the dangers of untrammelled development and the balance that needs to exist between economic growth and the environment.

Their success was in the decision that was made to preserve and maintain nine miles of linear park along the river from Ballsbridge almost to the Dublin mountains, with every community having a little share of it as stakeholders in ensuring its upkeep with Saturday-morning clean-ups.

The Dodder Valley principles and ethos, along with the local community and engagement, has also helped inspire others all over the country to take ownership of future developments of their own local environments. Most importantly, the rivers have shown themselves to be resilient in the face of urban pressures.

'What we have shown with the Dodder is a fantastic example that all you have to do is clean up the water and it will look after itself,' says Ken.

From where we've been chatting, it's just a short drive to Ken's house, where we get suited up in waders and boots. It's like a summer's evening and Herbert Park is busy with walkers, runners and the shouts and whistles of football matches. We get the predictable sideways glances as we walk along the footpath with our rods in hand, but as soon as we reach the river, all other distractions fade away.

The walkway is a quiet path distant from the park and the games, with only occasional walkers coming along here in the evening time. It's a secluded part, with a high wall behind us, but safe and well-lit. Besides, Ken reasons, the only other crazies who are out around here at this time are usually fellow anglers.

We come across a few throughout the evening, usually spinning for what trout they can catch.

Dusk is settling in now but the orange streetlights mean it will never be fully dark; however, that won't affect our fishing, Ken tells me, as the sea trout are used to the light.

A hatch of olive flies appears as we stand looking into the water and Ken ties an imitation on the dropper and a nymph on the point, a very similar set-up to earlier in the day with Des. 'We'll put on the flashier sea trout flies when it gets proper dark,' he tells me.

As we fish downstream, Ken tells me about his fascination with the sea trout. 'They're just so enigmatic; they're so shy and quiet and the great thing is there can be a lot more sea trout in the river or lake than you could possibly imagine.'

After spawning in fresh water, sea trout can spend up to four years around their place of birth before heading out to sea. For some, it's just a few months before returning, while for others, they can come back once a year to spawn – and can repeat this for eight years. As they get older, they feed less and less so they slip up on a flood, spawn and slip back to the ocean again without ever being seen by an angler.

Practically every day, whenever he is in Ireland and not working abroad as a fisheries scientist, Ken Whelan leaves his office at home and makes the short walk to the Dodder where he'll walk for a few hours along the banks of the river.

The effluent pipes that caused so much pollution decades ago are still there, but they're dry now, a testament to all that he, Ned and others such as Des Chew and Redmond O'Hanlon from the Dodder Anglers' Association fought tirelessly for. The

Haunted by Waters

empty pipes are a fitting tribute to what they've achieved and alongside them are the little streams, once milky and discoloured but running clear again.

'At this stage now I actually don't fish the Dodder very much,' Ken admits. 'But yet I still feel very much part of it because I walk it and see the trout rising. I get as much pleasure from actually watching the river as I used to when I was trying to take fish out of it.'

He remembers clearly, on one of his walks a few years ago, spotting salmon for the first time, and he couldn't believe what he was seeing.

'I looked across the river and I saw this shape in the water. I pinched myself and said, *that couldn't be a salmon?* Then I looked again, saw it was a salmon and then there was a second one and a third ... There were three salmon on the far side of the river while there were all these people standing beside me having their lattes and having a laugh, completely oblivious.

'And I said to them, "do you see anything in the water there?" "No," they said. "Look again," I told them. "Look very carefully." One guy had a set of sunglasses on and said, "Yes, I see the big fish!" Suddenly the fish moved closer to us and now they all could see the salmon and they had no idea those salmon were sitting below them. Then the bottom started to move and there were at least thirty or forty sea trout on the bottom of the river and I left those people ooh-ing and ahh-ing over what they had just seen.'

Ken's life's interest became a labour of love when he co-authored *Nomads of the Tides* with Chris McCully, detailing the biology of sea trout as well as the parts of Ireland where their history and fishing has been synonymous. After five years their work had been completed, an ode to, as well as an important reference work about, these unique fish.

Not surprisingly, perhaps, Ken's favourite places for sea trout are the smaller rivers of the north-west. He likes their intimacy, much like our own location on the Dodder, albeit vastly different in character. Paradoxically, he also relishes estuary fishing for sea trout, seeing in the wide expanse of water the greater challenge.

'It's really exciting because it's so difficult. It's a real lottery as to whether the sea trout will be in, and it depends on conditions, it depends on the tides, but if you get it right it can be fantastic. If you get it wrong, it can be a complete blank as well so it's a real challenge. There's nothing easy about it and I think that's why so few people actually bother – oh wait, sorry ...'

Talk of conditions has been cut short by an exciting turn of events. Ken is into a sea trout. His line tightens and with a small bend in the rod, I glimpse the silver body coming expertly towards us. One small jump and the fish confirms I'm witnessing a sea trout being caught under the darkness of the city lights.

'An incredible fish,' Ken says softly as he holds it in his wet hands. 'And a lovely size, about a half pound and in really very good condition.'

Ken must have caught thousands of sea trout in his lifetime and has been catching fish on the Dodder for more than six decades but still the sight of a fresh fish captures his imagination and wonder all over again.

'He's really fresh as you can see, he's absolutely perfect,

properly blue. He probably went out as a smolt in May and stayed in Dublin Bay for the last few months. I'd say he came up past the bridge this afternoon or on the tide yesterday evening and was just on his way back. Amazing …'

The fish goes safely back and we return to our gentle rhythms of casting, retrieving and casting again. A few minutes later and Ken is in again: this time it's a small salmon parr and within thirty minutes of starting we've completed a hat-trick of sorts on the Dodder. Brown trout, sea trout and now a small salmon parr.

'The whole way to Bohernabreena reservoir [a nineteenth-century reservoir at the foot of the Kiltipper mountains 12 km from Dublin] it's just replete with small fish,' says Ken. 'In reality, any pool you go to on any sort of half-normal evening, you will get eight to ten fish at least. A lot of them might very well be small but you could pick up some very good fish. Recently, on a walk up by Rathfarnham, I saw fish in the two- to three-pound bracket one evening. The light was just right and they were moving in one of the deeper pools, magnificent fish they were.'

The great thing about fishing with a fisheries biologist and expert angler is there is no shortage of questions you can throw at Ken and you will always learn something new in his company. This evening is like going to college, not in a didactic way, but in a generous, imparting fashion – Ken only answers the questions I ask.

I learn about the sea trout on the east coast of Ireland being fatter than those on the west coast ('they're better fed in the Irish Sea'); or how brown trout and rainbows can survive quite well in salt water; or that some sea trout in France are long-distance travellers who will venture as far as Denmark: 'almost like salmon in the distance they go'.

It's getting darker now and Ken says it's time to switch over to some 'proper' sea trout fishing. We replace the olive fly with something flashier, more appealing to the sea trout. The old adage about not starting sea trout fishing until you can't see across the field doesn't quite hold here but I know what Ken means, there's a certain depth to the darkness of the night now, despite the best efforts of the city.

'I'm a bit of an addict for night fishing,' he admits. 'I love night fishing whether it's for sea trout or bass or whatever – I just like fishing in the dark. I wouldn't mind at all fishing on though until one or two o'clock in the morning and certainly it's not unusual for me to fish late.

'What we're finding in all of the cities in Europe with the Water Framework Directive and the cleaner water, people are rediscovering waterways and discovering that they can be a great source of interest and enjoyment for themselves and for their children and grandchildren. You could be anywhere now and of course snags and tangles are part of that at night-time. It's seriously relaxing fishing though as everything's much slower.'

He strikes his rod up gently and stops mid-sentence.

'Excuse me,' he says almost apologetically as he's into another fish. 'This is a lovely silver fresh fish, very fresh … he's about 10 ounces to ¾ of a pound, just in after the tide and here we are, probably half ten at night. Can you see how silvery and pure he is, pure silver on the sides?'

We're at the bridge in Ballsbridge near the RDS now and in

the midst of the noise of a city at night, we watch the silver sea trout swim away. We're watching the story of the last fifty years of the Dodder and all the work that has been accomplished down through the generations. As we stand and watch the ripples in the water, I look across to the far bank at the car lights reflecting on the river. A double-decker bus drives past, empty save for one or two passengers. The lateness of the hour means that only the last few stragglers are out in the city tonight. That and two anglers fly fishing for salmon and sea trout. The river has called its last orders, time to call it a night.

10.
Kerry's Lough Currane and 'The Song of Amergin'

The summer had ended, the kids were back in school and the evenings were now about preparing school lunches and uniforms. Mornings were a blur between getting breakfasts ready, brushing stubborn hair to get it to stay down and school runs out the door. In between, travel to Dublin was still a constant and it was a juggling act between myself and my wife to keep it all running smoothly. But I somehow felt less pressured and agitated. Work-life balance hadn't changed and raising three kids hadn't got any simpler, but the simple act of committing to days of fishing, of focused acts for myself beyond the everyday had become experiences that had laid the foundations for the other parts of my life.

As the nights began to get longer, we were all missing the lazy, carefree summer days. The crops had been cut and the fields around our house lay bare, waiting to be ploughed. There was a real sense of the year beginning to close in. There was talk even from the kids of counting down to Halloween.

30 September, the last day of the season on most rivers and lakes around the country, had been and gone. I marked it as I usually do by one last trip to the Blackwater and Suir, but heavy rains in recent weeks meant the rivers were pretty much unfishable and I had to be content with a walk along the banks to pay homage to the season just gone. It had been the same nine months ago on the opening day when the waters were similarly

high and in many ways not much, and so much, had changed in the intervening time.

My experiences, the days out on the water, the hours spent casting in hope, had added to the sum of my time. The seasons had passed – I was a traveller in the year, the months of flux, the ups and downs – and still the river flowed unceasingly, pushing on to the ocean no matter what.

The summer season had been a difficult one weather-wise, despite fish being caught amidst the changeable weather conditions all across the country. Even though there had been some warmth in the days and some sunny breaks, it was still fickle and unpredictable. Rain when it did arrive could fall for a minute or an hour before quickly moving on. On the rivers, you had to time it right and, like so many other anglers, I didn't have that luxury most of the time.

The months had flown by – just like that – but still with so many highs, from fly fishing in the capital to catching my biggest bass and brown trout to date. I had been to Dublin, Cork, Waterford and, best of all, Connemara.

I would keep going until the last day though, I promised myself, experiencing everything I could that the fly fishing year had to offer. There were still twelve days left in the season on Lough Currane in south County Kerry, that iconic sea trout lake outside Waterville. There was still one more chance for a fish to be caught on the fly and for one last time to be on the water so that I could carry its memory with me into the barren winter months ahead.

I would hopefully be out chasing bass in October before the

water temperatures really dropped but I also knew 12 October on Lough Currane would bring the curtain down on the salmon and trout season. I wasn't ready to hang up the fly rod just yet.

I hadn't fished Lough Currane before and it was one more memorable fishery to tick off the list. Lying just outside Waterville on the Iveragh peninsula in County Kerry, at three and a half miles long and two miles wide, its reputation has been as a renowned sea trout fishery but there were plenty of posts on online forums on the decline of the fishery in recent years, and I decided I would need a good boatman and guide to put me on the fish. A few calls were made looking for the right person and Neil O'Shea's details were passed on. As luck would have it, he had a last-minute cancellation and I made my plans.

There was something gratifying about loading the car with fly fishing gear in October. I know of a few salmon anglers who will continue their season on into November, with weekend trips to Scotland, but for now, driving to Waterville, I was more than happy to have one last fly fishing opportunity.

Unlike Galway and Connemara, Kerry is not a county I know that well. The west of Ireland has always been more familiar because of my mother's family connection and the childhood holidays spent there. West Cork has now become our summer family destination of choice with the kids, while Kerry remains that bit further out.

There's a multitude of fishing available in the Kingdom, however, from the Feale near Listowel in the north, down to the Owenmore on the Dingle peninsula and across to the Laune and Killarney Lakes, and it should see me driving down more often.

I also wonder if my first experience of fishing in Kerry has left a lingering bad taste in my mouth. It was soon after my first time on the Suir when I caught my first brown trout with our neighbour Tom when he asked me if I wanted to join himself and his father, Joe, for a day's salmon fishing on the River Laune.

I jumped at the chance, not even knowing how one was supposed to catch a salmon, but Tom said he had a spare rod and flies which I could use. It would be an early start, he warned, hitting the road at 4 a.m. to be on the river just outside Killarney for 7 a.m. 'Even better,' I told him, knowing I wouldn't be sleeping much anyway with the excitement the night before. In the meantime, I had booked a lesson with Glenda Powell on the Blackwater to get some basics on double-handed casting with a fly rod. I was clumsy and inept but after an hour I had some notion of the basics and could cast a short line out. 'You'll do just fine,' Glenda had assured me. 'Now go catch a fish.'

In the car on the way down to Kerry, I had slept in the darkness of early morning, catching snippets of conversation between Tom and Joe about which were the best back roads to take. 'What's wrong with the motorway?' I muttered, but as a Dub I should have known better so I closed my eyes as we drove along the bumpy, winding, off-track roads.

It was mid-summer and the sun was shining brightly by the time we got to the river. I opened my eyes to be greeted by the sight of mist coming off the water, slowly disappearing into the morning sunshine. All around us were fields of cows and in the distance were the imposing MacGillycuddy Reeks rising out of the sky like a memory of some far-off land.

'Now, where's the box for the licence?' I heard Joe ask.

'Did the farmer not say he'd call down to the river and we'd give him the money then?' asked Tom. 'He said he'd be down after nine.'

'If he said that, fine with me,' Joe replied. 'Pull in here and we can fish from this stretch on.'

'What was that all about?' I asked Tom as I got out and stretched my arms and legs.

'Ah we just have to pay the farmer for a licence, that's all – the farmer who owns this land and has rights to the fishing. But he said he'd come down and we'll give him the money then, so no bother.'

We took the rods out from the boot of the car and tackled up. Joe, as usual, was ready in a minute and already fishing the water by the time myself and Tom followed behind him. I let Tom go in front so I could watch what he was doing and to see the spots he was targeting.

Not long after, we heard another car drive up and park alongside ours. Tom looked back quizzically when a man got out with a spinning rod, eyeing us suspiciously. He walked over to the bank to where we were targeting.

'Who said ye can be fishing here?' he said fiercely.

I shrugged my shoulders and turned to Tom.

'The farmer who owns the rights,' he replied sharply.

'Well, it's not his and ye're not allowed to be here.'

'Says who?' Joe called out angrily as he began to wade out of the river to confront the man.

'Says me and the others who have the fishing rights here.' His arms were on his waist defiantly now. He wouldn't be budging an inch.

'Well, we can sort this out easy enough,' said Tom calmly, taking out his phone and ringing the farmer who had given us permission to fish this stretch of the river.

'Ye, we're down here and there's someone else here telling us we can't fish,' said Tom into his phone ... 'Okay, we'll wait here so ...'

We waited in silence, standing in the field not saying anything until the farmer's 4x4 drove down. A small, squat man in wellies got out of the car and immediately the stranger beside us started shouting at him; soon the two were face-to-face raging at each other about 'rights', 'permissions' and 'the law'.

I thought it was going to end up in punches being thrown but instead the ranting and shouting continued in their strong Kerry accents, neither giving an inch, their eyes popping out and cheeks red. It was some sight and I turned away to look at the river as a reminder of why we were supposed to be there.

'And I thought fly fishing was meant to be a quiet, relaxing pastime,' I said, shaking my head. Tom laughed and then the farmer came over and said we could fish on. It appeared that some compromise of sorts had been worked out and Tom handed him the money for the licence.

'You'll be hearing from my solicitor and I'll have you in court!' the farmer shouted over to the other man as he got back into his car and drove off. So that was the compromise, I thought to myself.

'Come on, let's get back fishing,' said Joe impatiently.

Haunted by Waters

We climbed back down to the river only to be joined by the other angler, who promptly walked between us up on the bank and began casting his rod hooked with worms right next to our flies. On the far side was a wooden sign in large black and white letters: 'No spinning, no worming, private fishing only'.

I could see Tom and Joe were fuming, he was ruining the pool on purpose and trying to be as awkward as he could. We ignored him and kept fishing and eventually, having no luck, he reeled in and drove away. Tom shook his fist at him as his car left the field.

'What was that all about?'

'Something to do with fishing rights between local farmers,' Tom said. 'You get it down here sometimes.'

'So these rows are a regular occurrence when salmon fishing in Kerry?' I asked incredulously.

'Not regular, but it can happen alright. Let's hope the pool hasn't been ruined altogether by that idiot,' said Tom, casting a line out.

We fished on for the rest of the day without another sight or sound of the other fella and were at least left in peace to fish. Tom landed two grilse of about 5 lbs and I was captivated at seeing and holding a fresh salmon for the first time. But as we reeled in and loaded our rods and gear back into the car the talk wasn't of the fish caught but of the row from earlier that morning.

'We won't be coming back here again, unfortunately,' said Joe sadly.

'Aye, it's a nice bit of water alright,' said Tom. 'But they'd want to sort out their row first before I'd think of coming back down.'

It was a bit of excitement to liven up the day, I thought, a good story to tell when I got home. But I haven't been back to the Laune since and three months later Tom rang me to say the farmer needed a letter from us detailing what had happened that morning by the river as the case was going to court.

'That's fishing in Kerry for you,' said Tom, laughing down the phone.

Now I'm driving back down to the Kingdom, to Waterville, and wonder what's in store for me. I'm hopeful the only talk will be about the fishing.

I drive through Killarney and head for the Iveragh peninsula, a spectacular landscape of mountains and valleys immortalised in pictures, words and song. The landscape plays into the writings or maybe it's the other way around but either way each has fed off the other. The rugged terrain, the wildness of the countryside, the mountains looming large on the land, appearing in and out through the mists of the Atlantic that comes crashing into cliffs and jagged rocks – the romance of Ancient Ireland is all there in colour.

The rise in popularity of game angling during Victorian times saw Kerry, with its multitude of rivers and lakes to choose from, become a holiday destination for many visiting anglers from the late 1800s on. The development of the railways with lines reaching out to every corner of the remote headlands meant 'gentlemen fishermen' would arrive into Killarney and the south of the county from Dublin and England with their rods, lines and flies and a room and ghillie booked for weeks at a time.

North Kerry though was in stark contrast, it was a part of

Haunted by Waters

the county that didn't attract as many visitors. The terrain was different, flatter, less spectacular, more agricultural. Where football is played mainly in the south, in north Kerry hurling is dominant.

The north Kerry people eyed with suspicion, and not a little bit of wariness, the goings-on of the southerners who were kow-towing to the foreign visitors, opening up their waters and their land. The northerners were more circumspect.

That part of the county is also the centre of coursing in the country, one of the most controversial rural sports still in existence. Fascinated by the people and culture around it, I once produced a documentary for Radio Kerry on coursing, finding myself at one of the meetings near Ballyduff.

I got a fascinating insight into not only a niche sport, but also the culture and people that make up coursing in this part of Kerry.

As I drank pints with the crowd in a nearby bar afterwards, talk alternated between the experienced dogs and ones to watch, as well as the hurling. Not far from where we stood was Kilduff and the ferry across the bay to Clare while the other hurling strongholds of Limerick and Tipperary were only a few miles down the road. This was a far cry from Dingle, Killarney, tourists and the Gaelic football of the Kingdom.

Coursing, dogs, hunting, it was in contrast to the cosmopolitan, outward-looking southern part of the county. The tourists flocked to Killarney – it had its lakes and the spectacular Lady's View and MacGillycuddy Reeks. It had Dingle, the Gaeltacht areas, the Blaskets, Skellig Mhichíl, the Ring of Kerry, Waterville and the greatest footballers. Valentia Island, it was often pointed out to me, was where the first transatlantic cable was sent in 1866 and for a hundred years was where transatlantic cables were sent from. The postcards were from south Kerry.

Waterville was certainly no different. A small town on the Iveragh peninsula, you either approached it from Cahirciveen coming around via the Wild Atlantic Way, or perhaps most spectacularly, over the Ballaghisheen Pass and Glencar Valley through the MacGillycuddy Reeks themselves.

With only a narrow road and tour buses passing by it can be a challenging drive as you climb up the mountain trying to keep your eye on the road without being distracted by the spectacular peaks and also the valleys below. Then finally, you come over the pass and begin your descent, looking out onto the Atlantic Ocean and Waterville itself.

The village faces the Atlantic and Ballinskelligs Bay on one side, with Lough Currane's 2,500 acres on the other, tucked in behind it. It's a place of holiday homes, gift shops and restaurants all focused on the tourist market and the wide expanse of the bay in front of it. Of the many car rentals and coach tours that pass through Waterville as part of the Ring of Kerry, how many, I wonder, even know about the presence of Currane?

But Lough Currane is about more than just fishing. The history of Currane is a snapshot into Gaelic Ireland and the role salmon (and sea trout) played in the country's lore and history. Much as the River Drowes played an influential economic and historic part in the development of that corner of Ulster, so too Currane's role as a fishery was intertwined with the history of this area.

Haunted by Waters

As I drive into Waterville, my first port of call is not to the lake but instead I meet with Paddy Bushe, a poet and another Dub in exile, who has been living in Kerry for most of his life. Writing in Irish and English, he has won awards for his collections, with many focused on the Celtic mythology of the area. I wanted to go beyond the days of the Victorian anglers and tap into some of the Celtic myths that have wound themselves into the history of the place, etched into the fabric of the land and the psyche of the people.

A member of Aosdána, Paddy's first published collection was called *Poems with Amergin* and he is also organiser of a poetry festival in Waterville called the Amergin Solstice Poetry Gathering. Amergin was the Milesian bard who was part of the original settlers to Ireland and who, upon setting his right foot on the land at Ballinskelligs Bay proclaimed his poem, *The Song of Amergin*, and thus was also born Irish poetry and writing. In fact, Robert Graves, the celebrated English writer and poet, declared that, 'English poetic education should, really, begin not with the *Canterbury Tales*, not with the *Odyssey*, not even with *Genesis*, but with *The Song of Amergin*.'

> Mé gaoth ar muir
> Mé tonn díleann
> Mé glór mara
> Mé damh seacht gcomhrac
> Mé fiolar ar fhaill
> Mé deor drúchta faoin ngréin
> Mé áilleacht fáis

Mé torc ar ghail
Mé bradán sa linn
Mé loch ar mhá
Mé dún sléibhe
Mé suí eagna
Mé ga faoi bhua ag slaí sa chath
Mé dia a adhnann tine sa cheann

Am wind on sea
Am wave swelling
Am ocean's voice
Am stag of seven clashes
Am falcon on cliff
Am sunlit dewdrop
Am rarest of herbs
Am boar enraged
Am salmon in pool
Am lake in plain
Am fortified hilltop
Am learning's essence
Am sharpened spear dealing death
Am god who kindles fire in the head.

[Translation by Paddy Bushe]

I sat in Paddy's study with its floor-to-ceiling bookshelves, drawn constantly to the window looking out onto the sea where his house faced out from the cliff edge, Skellig Mhichíl visible in

Haunted by Waters

the distance, the clouds swirling around it, giving it a mystical air. The waves were making their way in from afar, a constant crescendo of white foam rising up and travelling along as far as the eye could see. It was an ever-changing sight of waves, light, clouds and rain that held me captive as I got caught up in its changing hues.

Despite the raw beauty of the Atlantic Ocean, a lot of the focus is also turned inland towards Lough Currane as well. It has always had a special place for the local community, providing as it did in years gone by food and commerce through its supply of salmon and sea trout. Even in Celtic mythology it was a place of renown, Paddy explained as he took me back through the centuries.

'The salmon and the lake have been central to the imagination of the original Gaelic invaders, the Milesians, who landed here in Ballinskelligs Bay, and Lough Currane – Lough Luíoch, as it was originally called – was a central place in that Gaelic imagination. The original *Song of Amergin*, having laid claim to the area, one of the lines is about conjuring salmon into the bay and the lake. Obviously people who settled here were very conscious that the salmon were central to the imaginative life, which is a reflection of the everyday and economic life. When you have a pool rich in salmon, it was very central to the place and it is reflected in the Celtic mythology.'

Later when the area was Christianised in the sixth century, Saint Finnian, a local monk, built important monastic settlements on Skellig Mhichíl and on Church Island on Lough Currane where the ruins of a twelfth-century church still stand. The story of Finnian's birth, Paddy tells me, is that salmon came out of the sunset into his mother's womb, while there's also stories of miraculous meals of salmon when Finnian had important visitors from the king or had beggars to feed. Symbolically as a life-giver, the salmon was hugely important throughout the centuries.

'I know nothing about fishing, but I love going out on the lake,' says Paddy. 'I keep a boat and regularly go out to Church Island. It's one of my favourite places. The remains there now are of a twelfth-century Hiberno-Romanesque church and it was obviously a church of some importance. The decorations around the doorway, if you look at what is left there today, and imagine what it was like when those carvings were new and fresh, are very elaborate.'

We fast-forward through the centuries and Paddy tells me how the name of the area changed to Waterville, reflecting the fact that colonial powers then owned the fishery and it was when the world-famous Butler's Pool came to be known.

When the Butler family moved into the area as customs and excise officials to keep an eye on the smuggling being done by the O'Connells in Derrynane, the perk they were given was the Currane fishery. They built their house beside the pool and called it Waterville House. All that separates the lough from the Atlantic is the short Currane River, the only source of entry for salmon and sea trout into the lough. It was the most productive stretch of fishing, where the fish could be easily caught, and so became an important commercial consideration over time.

Despite its isolation and stubborn independence, the area did eventually become more Anglicised, especially with the arrival of the first transatlantic cable to nearby Valentia Island in 1858.

Haunted by Waters

Within a decade, telegraphing between America and Britain had become more popular and more common, with a cable station being built and forty workers being employed, along with their families, in a mini colony in the area.

Valentia Island and its surroundings of Waterville and Lough Currane were slowly but surely opening up and with it came the gentry whose main pursuits were fishing and shooting. Coupled with the rise in popularity of game angling in the Victorian era, fly anglers began to arrive in numbers, around which the ghillieing culture of locals guiding the visiting fishermen began to develop.

The Butler Arms Hotel opened in 1884 on the edge of Waterville and quickly became the centre of the fishing tourism. It was a place where the ghillies came each morning to be assigned their clients for the day while later that evening the bar would be the place for tall tales and small truths as the paying guests got to recount their exploits with the rod. To this day, the bar is still known as the Fishermen's Bar.

'Even when I came here,' remembers Paddy, 'there was a little hatch in the bar where the clients apparently used to send drinks out to their ghillies who were in what was a fairly basic bar on the outside. There were whole families – almost dynasties – of ghillies and it was very much part of the social and economic fabric of the place.'

The hotel was built the same year the Commercial Cable Company set up its cable station in Waterville and cemented the role tourists and visitors would have in the place. Over the next five decades, some very famous people came to the area to fish, from Walt Disney to John Steinbeck and Charlie Chaplin.

Chaplin nearly didn't even get a room, being told the hotel was full on his arrival. But when he was finally recognised, the owner's private suite was made available. It was to be the first of multiple summers that Chaplin fished and stayed with his family.

It's a long stretch from the Celts to Saint Finnian to Charlie Chaplin and not many lakes can lay claim to such a pedigree. I drove on from Paddy Bushe's house, thanking him for the tea, his lines of poetry still echoing in my ears as I headed up the road to Currane to meet my ghillie, Neil O'Shea, for the rest of the day.

The rain was beginning to come down heavily as I pulled up by the lakeshore. The mountains surrounding Currane were shrouded in clouds and Church Island was a blur in the distance. The wind was whipping up a swell and the waves were beginning to rise up across the lake.

'How about we go in here for a minute?' said the approaching man in his lilting Kerry accent. 'I'm Neil, by the way, and welcome to Lough Currane.'

He led the way to a small hut nearby where, once inside, the rain could be heard bouncing off the corrugated roof.

'This is a soft day around these parts I suppose?' I said, unzipping my jacket. A gas heater in the corner was giving off a stuffy heat. Neil boiled the kettle and we sat down for a cup of tea.

'Might be best to let the wind and rain die down a bit before we head out,' he said, handing me the hot cup. 'It's some day for fishing.'

I told Neil about my visit to Corrib earlier in the year in similar conditions and he nodded. 'Aye, things are changing alright.'

It wasn't just the weather either. I had been reading reports of anglers struggling to catch from Currane in recent years and that sea trout numbers had been in decline. What had once been a jewel of Irish fisheries appeared to be badly damaged. Inland Fisheries Ireland had announced that research was being carried out into the reasons why but for many it was obvious – from fish farms in the bay to the wider problem of climate change.

The rise of aquaculture in recent years has been a contentious issue. The open-net pens (cages in the sea with a net on top for farming fish), first set up in the bays around Connemara in the 1980s, were the reason most believed the sea trout runs collapsed in that area and in the west of Scotland, where fish stocks were similarly impacted.

Wherever the open-net pens have been located, the sea lice and discharge from the fish farms have devastated the wild salmon and sea trout, and anglers and environmental campaigners have been fighting vigorously for the government to introduce a more robust regulatory regime.

The knock-on effect is not just environmental either. For ghillies like Neil O'Shea, who is a fourth-generation ghillie, declining fishing impacts directly on their livelihoods.

'My father was a ghillie, my grandfather was a ghillie, my great-grandfather was a ghillie, and on my mother's side my uncle and my grandfather were also ghillies,' Neil tells me proudly. Fishing on Lough Currane provided a full-time job for him and his descendants from January to October, going back through the generations.

'In the early parts of January they'd troll for salmon and sell the salmon,' he explains. 'Then they'd have clients from March on. The whole business generally would be repeat clients; mainly English retired people spending two to three weeks here and fishing every day. There was a Captain Russell who would come for three weeks and then a Dublin farmer after him for three weeks. It was fierce busy and was all based around the Butler Arms Hotel. My uncle told me that at one stage there was twenty-five ghillies working out of it.'

There's a certain sense of being powerless, of events being beyond one's control now though. In the grand scheme of things, what can you really do against multi-billion-euro industries and global climate change? Outside the hut on the lake there is still fishing to be had and while the numbers of fish just aren't the same, they can still be caught, though not as plentifully as in years gone by. We can all hanker after the 'good old days' but it won't change the situation we're in at present.

Sea trout over 10 lbs are still recorded annually, Neil tells me and he explains how the water and weather impact greatly on the fishing, with the salmon and sea trout runs dependent on the water levels of the Currane River bringing the fish in from the sea. They can then pass through the lough to access the upper lakes of Lough Derriana, Lough Na Mona, Lough Cloonaghlin, Lough Na Huisce (Iskanamacteery), and Capal Lake (Isknagahiny).

Neil reckons there's at most half a dozen ghillies that would be full time with about ten in total working out of Currane. It's a far

Haunted by Waters

cry from the peak days of twenty-five operating out of the Butler Arms and as he reminds me, back then the guiding was all done by rowing as well. It wasn't until the 1960s that the first of the engines arrived.

Engines or not, ghillieing or private boats, fly fishing has been the one constant on the lake with a proud and long tradition of it.

'It was always part of it,' says Neil. 'People always came here for the fly fishing. It's been there as long as anglers came here. It is the most effective way to catch sea trout.'

As we talked about fishing, the rain continued to pound on the roof above. I hoped it would ease off before we headed out.

'I'm giving no guarantees on a day like this,' says Neil, glancing out the window. The lake is only a hundred yards away, just about visible through the wind and rain. 'The residents might be reluctant to come up though. Desperation stakes are hitting now, you see. For sea trout, settled conditions are better. At this time of year the wind can be very light and you can have success, but today? Hopefully we can get one of them to make a mistake.'

Neil is a realistic optimist, born for the lake, like his father, father's father, and father's grandfather before him. As a full-time guide you're at the mercy of the weather, the fishing and the visiting anglers, tough enough at any one time. He knows the lake – its whims, every nook and cranny, drifts and likely holding spots in every type of weather and conditions – but it is getting tougher.

The constancy of the seasons has gone and the weather can swing from one extreme to another. Currane might not suffer as much as the rivers in droughts like the one in 2018, but like everywhere else, the numbers of fish are just not there any more and are getting harder to catch on the fly.

If the weather is a washout, there's nothing Neil or the booked anglers can do except sit it out and look forlornly at the water through rain-soaked glasses. That or console themselves with the bottom of another glass in the Fishermen's Bar in the Butler Arms.

You learn to be stoic, working in what is a precarious enough job dependent so much on external factors for your livelihood. With all the problems of recent years, Neil and the other full-time ghillies would be forgiven if they decided enough was enough and threw in the towel. Like the three generations before him, however, he won't. You have to live with the conditions – isn't that what previous generations did after all? – and do what you can.

The days of anglers visiting for weeks, or even months, may be over, and the days of abundant catches no more, but it doesn't mean the sport is dead. There are still regulars who have their days booked the same time each year and who will come regardless. They are the anglers who come from all over the world who want to fish in peaceful, rugged, scenic surroundings with the chance of catching a salmon or sea trout on the fly.

We finish our tea and zip up our rain jackets tight. It's still raining but I've come all this way and while Neil might not be hopeful, with a fly on the water you never know.

The boat powers out from the bay into the teeth of a strong wind, the rain stinging the skin on my face. I wish I could write about marvelling at the scenery all around us but in truth it was hard to see past the driving rain and rising waves. The boat pitched up and down as Neil sought out shelter near an island. Finally he found a spot and cut the engine. We cast towards the stony shore and I realised it was Church Island in front of us. Through the sheets of rain I could just about make out the walled ruins of the church.

This was where Saint Finnian had come all those centuries ago and before that, Amergin and his people. Now here in the twenty-first century, all that stood was a crumbling wall and a poem passed on through the ages. But it was enough to build upon, enough to keep believing in the cycle of life.

The ancients were more in tune with nature and the world around them than we will ever be, but when they came to Lough Luíoch all those millennia ago, they believed in the same thing that Saint Finnian believed in, along with the Gaelic chieftains and the Charlie Chaplins of this world. It's what Neil O'Shea and his family before him, like other families in the area, have been doing, and will continue to do. We all breathe deeply of the waters and what they have to offer.

'For many years when I was here it was just the physical beauty of the lake that attracted me,' Paddy Bushe recalled earlier that morning. 'It's extraordinarily beautiful and peaceful. But when you're out there, if you can imaginatively enter into a place it can be incredibly stimulating. You imagine and try to get into the mind of the person who founded the monastery, even imagine hearing the chants of the monks.'

Despite the changes being wrought upon our planet, on the fish in the bay and out in the wider oceans, hidden here in the valley on the lake we kept casting and fishing, some would say in a forlorn hope, but we did it anyway, shivering wet and cold from the wind and the rain.

Unlike days gone by there was no salmon for us that day, just one small sea trout, hard won in the atrocious conditions but welcome nonetheless. My final fish of the season. I held him for a moment, his silver body one of shining hope, then watched him swim off into the dark, choppy waters.

As we rowed back to the shore, I wanted to take it all in one last time. The lake, the island, the mountains, the boat, the fishing rod lying across my lap, even the wind and the rain stinging my face. I felt alive in this place, out here on the water.

I thought of my promise to myself to get out fishing more and the greatest satisfaction of all has been sticking to it, giving myself the permission and time to make it happen. It may have only been twenty days in total but it has been energising for all those other days when real life is going on. The travel to Dublin for work; deadlines; the daily filling up of the email in-box; phone calls, texts and messages; family commitments … the routine of daily life has been interrupted every so often with these fishing trips and I feel grateful and better for it.

I admire and envy the ghillies whose life is all about the fish and the fishing, but theirs is not a bucolic existence either and their struggles are the same as mine and everyone else's. Their passion is their life, however, and while many of us cannot do the same, we can seek to incorporate more of what we love doing into our days, when we can. Life still awaits me when I jump off the boat and drive back to Tipperary, but I do so with a different

Haunted by Waters

perspective and a quiet sense of contentment of who I am and what gives me fulfilment, and that is what matters the most.

11.

End of the Line
at Ballyduff

I drive away from Lough Currane and close the door on another fishing season. I might get out once or twice for some bass fishing around Dungarvan if the weather is mild, but for the salmon, sea trout and brown trout, it's time to hang up the rods for the winter.

I concentrate hard on the winding road around the Iveragh peninsula, the rain pounding in now from the Atlantic. The wipers are on full speed but they're struggling to keep the windscreen clear. 'Must be mad,' I laugh, and smile to myself, exhilarated from the day's fishing and knowing I'd do it all again in the same conditions in a heartbeat if I could.

It's beginning to get dark now, and Halloween and the start of winter is little more than two weeks away. The clocks will be going back and the nights drawing in, the shutters being closed at home earlier and earlier each evening. There's something comforting though about a blazing, warm fire, the logs crackling in the flames as you sit on the sofa feeling the warmth and heat while outside the cold sets in. I'll still be thinking, reading and writing about fly fishing in the coming weeks and months, you can't shake free of it entirely.

I pass through Killarney and drive over the River Laune, wondering when I'll next be in Kerry. As the miles tick past I start to make a mental note of the places I want to fish next year. Slowly the places on my list are being ticked off. I still have to get to the

Moy in County Mayo and I'll go back to the Drowes, though not perhaps on 1 January. There's the famous Galway Salmon Weir, and there's also Lough Mask, Sheelin, Derg, Costello and Fermoyle, Caragh and Carrowmore … so many places still to visit and savour. Unfortunately the glory days of many of these fisheries has been and gone and I want to fish them mainly because of their history, their place in Ireland's rich fly fishing culture that is beginning to fade.

Passing through the quiet streets of Mallow, only an hour from home, I decide that in the closed season of winter I will write about the people and places that make up Ireland's fly fishing past; of the people I've met and fished with. It will be a project to keep me busy and a way to try and preserve some of our fly fishing past.

It will also be a way to jot down my experiences from a wonderfully fulfilling year. I have been right across the country, from Donegal to Cork, from Dublin to Galway, and visited places I had never been to before. I've experienced at first hand the Irish fly fishing culture that is hanging on, just about, in these remote rural places and met some of the people for whom it is nothing short of a way of life.

But I have also discovered something about myself. I had set a goal and followed it through, I had pushed myself out of my comfort zone, out onto the road to travel to new places and meet new people. Paradoxically, in the flowing lakes, rivers and the sea I found a stillness, rooted in nature, that has helped ease my internal tensions and proved to be a barrier to the pressures from the external world. I feel stronger, with a new outlook not focused just on work or the mundane and quotidian, but seeing the beauty and joy in the simplicity of casting a fly in far-flung corners of Ireland. I realise that, for too long, I have been fearful of going out and experiencing what I didn't know, staying only in the corner that I knew best, internalising what should be rather than experiencing what is.

Onto Mitchelstown and the M8 motorway, I'm just thirty minutes from home and I decide to call someone I haven't seen for some time, someone whose story is indelibly linked to their place on the river and of pursuing a dream.

A gravelly Welsh accent answers and the call is short and to the point, as always. No problem, I can visit next week. 'I'm not going anywhere,' he tells me before hanging up. I see the signs for the Cahir exit – I'll be home in minutes. I'll be taking down my rods and putting them away in my fishing cupboard but I smile to myself, knowing I won't be leaving fly fishing behind me altogether.

'How did it go?' my wife asks as I come in the door. The kids run over in their pyjamas wanting to know if I have pictures of fish to show them.

'Just the one,' I say, showing them the sea trout, which the boys agree was small and I was right to put back.

'When will you bring us?' they ask expectantly.

'Next year, guys, next year, the season is over for another year,' I tell them. 'But don't forget, there's the fly fishing fair in November that we'll be going to.'

Their faces light up. It's our annual day trip together to Galway to the Irish fly fishing fair where they get to buy flies and other fishing gear before running on the beach across from the hotel and then finishing up with a McDonald's on the way home. It's our day out together and a highlight in the run-up to Christmas.

'So no more fishing then?' Trina asks.

'Well, not quite,' I reply as I put my rod and bag away. 'You see, I had this idea ... I want to write about fly fishing in Ireland, the people and the places.'

'Any excuse,' she laughs, knowing it will keep me happy and distracted over the coming winter.

A week later and I find myself in a dark and damp stone room. The doors are locked, the lights are off and packed boxes are piled into the corners. Dust and cobwebs are gathering in the windows and there's an empty lifelessness to the place. But the pictures of salmon and fishermen are still hanging on the walls, and the few rods still lying around the room belie a different past.

'Mind your step there walking through,' advises the man in the Welsh accent. He is small and stooped but still walks with a purpose, knowing every nook and cranny of this old building. 'Where you're standing used to be the ticket office for Ballyduff railway station. There is the original ticket hatch, and over there was the waiting room, the fireplace, and the toilets for ladies and gents. I turned it into a drying room but we kept some of the original fixtures from the station.'

Blackwater Lodge, resting on a hill a few fields above the mighty Blackwater River on the Cork–Waterford border, is no ordinary fishing lodge, as you quickly gather when you first walk in. But then its owner, Ian Powell, is no ordinary lodge owner either. Both have remarkable tales to tell which became entwined to make Blackwater Lodge one of Ireland's premier salmon fisheries in the 1980s and '90s.

Sadly though, after nearly thirty years Ian was forced to close the lodge in 2015 and all that now stands is the remarkable building and the ghosts of fishing past. Close your eyes and you can almost hear the hum of excited conversation in the now-empty bar; breathe in the smoke-filled air of a time gone by when whiskey, pints, cigarettes or a cigar were the staple after dinner. But most important was the company of fellow salmon anglers as they reviewed the day, the ones that got away and the lucky so-and-so who had caught three fish on their first outing.

As we leave the 'drying room' to head into the main part of the lodge, I'm struck by the fact that I'm standing in the footsteps of Irish rural history. Long before there was a fishing lodge, this was the Ballyduff railway station, one stop on the Mallow to Rosslare line, connecting commerce and people to the towns and communities of south Munster, but most importantly to the boats in Wexford heading for England.

Built in 1872, rural railway stations such as Ballyduff were an important lifeblood for rural Irish villages connecting the people with the wider world of Cork, Waterford and England. But in the first half of the twentieth century, with cars becoming more accessible, the railway lines between the villages of rural Ireland were becoming increasingly empty. The decision was finally taken in 1966 to close Ballyduff railway station (along with so many other country stations) and its imposing grey granite building lay empty atop the hill overlooking the quiet village.

There it would have lain derelict and crumbling, its windows boarded up, a reminder of a distant past, but for the fact that it was situated only a few fields away from the Blackwater River, and so this particular abandoned station was to have a different story.

In the 1960s, a local had the idea to turn the old railway station into a lodge linked to fishing on the river beside it, and Blackwater Lodge was born. It was a fishery unlike any other, with a railway station and platform walls still visible and running through its centre. It struggled in its early years, however, and it seemed that what it was crying out for was an owner with as unique a background as the building to bring it fully to life.

When you're a rocker and your nights are taken up playing support to Pink Floyd, it can be hard to understand where salmon fishing would fit in. But then, Ian Powell is a man of many contradictions and has lived the life less ordinary.

How many others would buy a fishing lodge in Ireland having only seen it once before; who would give up their well-paid job in Strasbourg and get their parents to sell their house in Wales to move over too; who would start their life over at forty-two, arriving in Ireland on Christmas Eve without knowing a soul and suffering through minus 16 degrees at night?

'I always had in the back of my mind that I'd like to own a fishing hotel,' he tries to explain. 'Initially my dreams were to be a famous rock star, owning a castle and estate in Scotland which I would retire to.'

The rock star dreams faded away as did the castle, but he still dreamed of a fishing hotel and it was a constant in his thoughts. He finished his chemical engineering degree (while supporting the likes of Pink Floyd at night) and entered the working world. Although the hair was shorter and the guitar gathered dust, the fishing dream did not.

'I had a book which was called *How to Buy Your Own Hotel*, and this was always in my briefcase so whenever I was travelling, I would be studying this and looking at case scenarios, learning what was involved in running a hotel.

'I was also a subscriber to *Trout & Salmon* magazine and when I got my copy, I would devour it from cover to cover. There were two things I looked at particularly: one was the fishing reports and the other was the classified advertisements for fishing and businesses.

'The owner of the lodge here on the Blackwater used to put in reports in the magazine, and for some reason I was very taken by them. I couldn't explain why I had an interest in it, but I used to follow it all the time and I always had the Blackwater in my head.

I was heading off to Scandinavia for a week to visit companies up there and I had my spanking new copy of *Trout & Salmon* with me. I was on the plane – in business class, of course, with my briefcase and all that – and I opened my *Trout & Salmon*. I started looking through my usual bits at the back of the magazine and what did I see but Blackwater Lodge was for sale. Ding ding, bells started ringing for me there and then.'

He still hadn't actually been to the river or even visited that part of Munster but now was his chance to seize the opportunity and when he came back from his business trip he booked the phone call to 'Ballyduff 35'.

All of the phone calls for the area went into the local post office which was in the village. The postmaster would sit down at a board with sockets on it and put jack-plugs into holes when you wanted to get through to somebody.

Getting through eventually to speak to the owner, it all came crashing down when he was told, 'Sorry but it's already been sold to a Welsh couple', who were going to take it over at the start of the following season. The disappointment was crushing but the owner asked him over for some fishing to at least visit the place.

Later that summer he flew into Dublin on a Friday for the weekend and soon afterwards set eyes on the majestic Blackwater for the first time in person. He was disappointed at what might have been, and enjoyed the scenery and the fishing, but in his mind he moved on.

'There were good catches of salmon on the river and I thought it had a lot of potential but as it stood it was sold and the new owners were taking it over at the start of the new year. It was a dead end as far as I was concerned, so I was back to square one and I didn't really think about it anymore.'

Until, that is, he noticed after a few months of the new fishing season that the ads for fishing at the lodge went back to the style of the original owner. Something was up, he thought, and he booked another call to Ballyduff to find out. Sure enough, the new owners had paid their deposit and started on 1 February but by the end of March they had had enough and scarpered, leaving the deposit behind.

'We'd better start talking,' was Ian Powell's reply – the flame was still flickering and he flew over again to begin negotiations. The dream was one step closer to becoming a reality.

'You've already got the deposit so you can knock that off the asking price,' was his opening salvo before he got some more knocked off the price and he finally agreed to buy Blackwater Lodge, a few associated bungalows and its single salmon beat for £125,000.

'I couldn't afford to do it myself so my parents decided that they would sell their house and move over here with me. I was an only child and had flown the nest and I was abroad for eight years so they bought the bungalow next to me and with the rest of their money my father came into the business with me.'

The Welsh Powells had moved over lock, stock and barrel leaving everything behind; there was no way they weren't going to make it work. Ian arrived to pick up the keys on Christmas Eve 1985, but it was to be just before the start of the season on 1 February that he was able to access the main Lodge building.

'The doors opened on 31 January and there I was, knowing absolutely nothing about running a lodge, a bar, or a fishery. I'd only just got the keys, I didn't even know where the switch was to turn on the central heating – and it was minus 16 at night! Fortunately, I was very blessed because there were two women who worked here, one who did housekeeping and reception and the other who was the cook, and they were absolute gems as they guided me through the initiation of getting used to things. But there was so much I had to learn.'

There were French anglers already booked in for the new season and an existing client list that he could at least call upon. He was brimming with ideas and saw only the potential. One of the first things was to get new maps of the river and the fishing beats so anglers knew where they were going and where they needed to fish. The best way, he decided, was to hire an aeroplane to fly over the river while he hung out of it with his camera, getting the best shots.

'I had this old lady who was about eighty and who flew me in her two-seater aircraft out of Cork airport, starting upstream at Mallow, working our way down to Ballyduff. And I still to this day have the folders with the original photographs that I took from the plane.'

It was perhaps typical of Ian Powell that he wasn't going to do things by halves, even if it meant going up in a two-seater being flown by an eighty-year-old.

Even his log books, the records of fish caught each day by the anglers, describing the lure or fly, the river conditions, the beat, and the size of fish caught, were to catch his attention and were turned into something different.

'Hold on a minute while I get the books – and some beers,' he says, jumping up from the dusty old couch in the bar where we sit looking down onto the sweep of the Blackwater. A few minutes later and Ian returns with drinks, glasses and, more importantly, the Blackwater Lodge fishing books.

The record books of a fishery are a vital part of its survival. Salmon anglers thrive on information about accurate catch rates, and the more detailed and the further back they go, the better. After all, who wants to book a week's salmon fishing in April if there have been no fish caught that month in the last ten years? Or what about the overall catch rate on the fishery beats? Have they been dropping or going up at certain times of the year, and how many anglers were the catch rates based on?

Such questions – and their answers – in the record books are key to salmon anglers, helping to make up their minds about where and when they go fishing. I open the pages of the first book and see the year 1964 written large in blue biro at the top.

Surprisingly, the records of fish being caught were very low in the 1960s. Just thirty-seven in April, eleven in May, fourteen in July, forty-five in August, although there would have been very little fishing with little to no access to the river, Ian Powell points out.

'Most of the local anglers would have been trout fishermen and not salmon fishermen, which is a historical thing, you know – Anglo-Irish landlords and all that.'

Thankfully it's changed and salmon fishing, while still seen as the more expensive sibling of fly fishing, is open and accessible right across the country. By the time of Powell's arrival, boundaries had broken down, but the actual records of fish caught were patchy to say the least.

From 1986 on that was all to change and Ian Powell was meticulous about capturing every record: of rods gone out, fish caught and by what method. What's more, the numbers also reflected the changing times and changing seasons and flicking through the pages, you get a sketched history of the lodge's fortunes.

From 1980 to '85, the six-year average for total fish caught was 410. In Ian's first season, the number for the season shot up to 700. More anglers, more fishing, more salmon being caught. The numbers didn't lie.

'When anglers went out the door, they were getting to where they were supposed to be going much more quickly and easily, getting onto the river much faster, spending more time fishing the river properly because they had good advice on what to be doing. So it became far more productive.'

What also stands out, as you flick through the pages, is how dramatically the style of the entries changes, going from standard biro writing to, just a few months later, a magnificent calligraphic font, all flourishes and long tails. It makes you stop, read and appreciate the catches even more.

'One thing with salmon fishing is it's steeped in history,' says Ian proudly. 'There's this ambience and sophistication about it. And even something simple like the catch records merit being portrayed in a more elaborate way.'

The first entry records a certain 'I. Powell' as catching the lodge's first salmon – a 9-lb fish on 2 February in temperatures of minus 6. He reckons he was also the first to catch a fish on the entire river that year and it's there marked down for posterity as the first catch under his ownership.

While Blackwater Lodge wasn't the Scottish castle estate in the Highlands, for Ian Powell it was the next best thing.

'It was where I always wanted to be in life,' he says in a moment of contentment. 'There was a whole host of challenges, but it was a very exciting and extremely busy time.'

The improvements had their desired effect over the coming years and pretty soon Blackwater Lodge became a successful Irish salmon fishery, growing very quickly. Numbers of visiting anglers were increasing year-on-year and month-on-month, coming from Ireland, the UK, Europe and the United States. By the turn of the century, after fifteen years in business, turnover was five to six times what it was when he started. He'd even found a wife and was to start a family around life at Blackwater Lodge.

Older anglers always talk about the golden days, the 'I remember when' stories of when salmon were just waiting to be caught. While the 1980s or '90s wouldn't match the earlier decades, they were still years that Ian Powell remembers fondly and it was a time that, if he could have it back again, he would gladly revisit.

At the height of the season, the place was 'humming', the bar in the centre of the lodge packed with anglers, relaxing amongst friends, chatting about the day's fishing, the salmon caught and the ones that got away.

'I don't want to say, you know, "Oh I was responsible for what happened on the Blackwater", but that's what a lot of other people's impressions would be, that it wasn't until the lodge really started motoring under my management that the Blackwater really became a salmon fisherman's destination within Europe. It was certainly one of the best rivers in Ireland and probably in Europe as well.'

The broad windows look down over the river and the Blackwater Valley, a perfect backdrop to the anglers' conversations. All around the walls are paintings of salmon fishing scenes, and behind the bar is one of Ian and a group of anglers locked deep in conversation around a salmon fly that Ian is holding.

Over their pints, this group of four men are lost to the world, focused only on the colours and make-up of the fly. What is its provenance? Who tied it? Was this the one that caught the 20-pounder this morning? Will it work tomorrow? Or should they try something different? The conundrum of fly fishing after-hours was caught in that moment between the anglers who will spend a lifetime examining with deeply held conviction such life-affirming problems.

In another corner, above the fireplace, is a painting of Ian Powell lying on the grass beside the riverbank, arms outstretched, with a salmon in the net beside him. It's a rare moment of victory for the salmon angler, both fish and man exhausted after their battle.

'That scene was painted from a photograph,' he explained. 'It was early season, near Ballyhooly Bridge, six miles upstream of Fermoy. The water was high and I was out fishing more in hope than expectation when I saw a guy on the bridge with his camera taking pictures. He soon came over to me, in a terrible state.

'He was on a magazine assignment to take pictures of the Blackwater, including a salmon, and had seen nothing all day. "Can you help?" he asked me as he started snapping away. No pressure then! I didn't rate my chances, I told him, but he badly needed a picture of a salmon.

'There was a piece of calm water amongst the high currents that I spied and thought might hold a salmon, so I cast out to it and almost immediately – wham! – the lure was pulling hard away from me. I struck, and knew I was into a good fish. The only problem was trying to get near the bank to land it. The water was pulsing under the arches of the bridge and it was dangerously high to get too near the water.

'Meanwhile, the photographer couldn't believe his luck – and neither could I – "I just need the picture of you with the salmon now," he tells me. There was a narrow ledge of rocks near the edge that I thought I could use to get closer to the fish and I made my way slowly across. The white torrents of water flew past my feet as I struggled to keep my balance while holding the rod and trying to reel in this Atlantic salmon that was fighting me and the current.

'"You hold the net," I told the other guy. "You're going to land it for me." "But I've never netted a salmon in my life," he said. "Well, you are now," I replied, shoving the net into his hand as he made his way onto the rocky sill beside me.

'It was a nerve-wracking few minutes, but finally I got the fish near to us. After a few more half-hearted runs, the fish had been subdued. "Get ready," I said. "Now, put the net under him." The fish was landed in the net safely and I couldn't believe it. We just had to manoeuvre our way back onto dry ground and when I jumped onto the grass I grabbed the net, marvelling at the 20-lb fresh salmon before us. All I could do was collapse on the ground beside it. The struggle, the battle, the fish caught. I had done it. Of course, in between catching his breath, the photographer began snapping away again and one of the images was what you see on the wall here turned into a painting.'

The sparkle of energy in the telling of stories from those days brings a lightness to his voice, and you can tell how much delight he got from building up the lodge into something that was talked about around Ireland, the UK and Europe and how salmon anglers would come back year after year, staying for weeks on end. The fishing was good, the craic was mighty and the tall tales were all part of the day.

Everything has its season, though, and while there may have

been offers to sell up, moving on was never really a consideration. The turn of the century came, he had been fifteen years in Ireland and on the Blackwater, but dark clouds were just around the corner.

'We invested everything that was coming in to improving the place – in hindsight, we should have been paying off the debts,' he says ruefully.

When foot-and-mouth struck in 2001 it was to be the start of a number of crises that would lead to a downward spiral. The outbreak started on a farm in the UK in February that year and soon it was apparent that it had spread, with fifty cases a week being reported. The authorities had not been able to contain the disease and Ireland's worst fears were confirmed when it too reported its first case on a County Louth farm.

For a country like Ireland, reliant so much on agriculture, it could have turned into a disaster. But the authorities were quick into action. Animals were slaughtered, quarantines put in place, sports matches from internationals to junior club games were cancelled, along with horse racing and greyhound meetings. The movement of people around the countryside was severely curtailed and for fishery owners like Ian, it was a monumental disaster. All country sports, including fishing, were banned until finally, the worst of it was over by the summer.

For Blackwater Lodge – and so many others right around the country involved in tourism and public events – it would be a long time before the recovery actually took place. On top of that, 9/11 happened in September and the numbers of visiting Americans shrank drastically. 2001 was a year to forget.

'We were closed down from February until May and there

was no fishing whatsoever, no access across farmland to go to the river – completely, completely closed,' Ian recalls. 'Then we opened up on a limited basis with disinfection mats and all this kind of thing so we still had a lot of restrictions that really hit us hard. Then 9/11 happened and all of those things hit in the same year.'

It was only the beginning of the decline, however. It wasn't just the visitors that were dropping; salmon numbers were in trouble as well. A government advisory group had warned that the salmon population would fall to 'catastrophic' levels if driftnet fishing was not banned immediately, and while inshore commercial fishermen were offered €25 million in compensation to quit in 2007, it wasn't to be the panacea many hoped for and salmon fishing was to continue to struggle in the years afterwards.

'There was a build-up of concern about driftnets and salmon stocks,' Ian explains. 'There was already quite a lot of worry about what was happening until we got the nets taken off – and then we went straight into the recession, which whacked us again. It was a gradual decline after that.'

Selling up and moving back to Wales to run a B&B with some sea trout fishing crossed his mind more than once, but ultimately he never was quite able to leave the Blackwater behind.

'I wasn't trying to make a fortune. Basically, you make a living, not a fortune, when you do something like this.'

He had invested so much of his life, career and dreams into the place. Was hanging on, hoping things would turn around, the answer, though? When the international banking system nearly collapsed and the Irish property bubble burst with it, the ensuing recession killed off any chance of survival. People and the economy were doing their best to keep above water; salmon fishing was not high on many people's agendas.

Amidst the recession and the business troubles, his marriage ended in divorce and then, if he thought it couldn't get any worse, he was diagnosed with lung cancer. A lifelong smoker, he wasn't altogether surprised, and despite having tried and failed to quit on numerous occasions, he didn't see any point in giving up now.

He was about to turn seventy, he was living alone, his fishery was in serious financial trouble, and now he wasn't even sure how long he had to live. That was when he made the decision to finally close the lodge. The banks had been knocking and calling, looking for debts to be paid off, but without any customers, how did they expect the loans to be cleared? He couldn't delay the inevitable anymore. He needed to focus on his health, to stop worrying about the lodge. His immediate health and future had to take centre stage.

'I wasn't even sure if I was going to be alive coming into the following season,' he says. 'If I had been taking money off people it wouldn't have been the right thing to be doing, if I wasn't sure that I was going to be there and be able to be running the place in the way that I would always have wanted to see it run. So I decided that was the time to stop.'

In 2015, Ian Powell officially announced the closure of Blackwater Lodge. He had nearly made it to thirty years, it would have been a neat bookmark, but life isn't like that. It gives you good times and shakes you up, and all you can do is go along for the ride.

'It was soul-destroying because you spend thirty years of your life building something which was a dream, achieving something that was very successful in its time, which provided a very nice lifestyle, and a very good injection of revenue into the local economy in the valley and Ballyduff in particular, between leasing beats and people coming in and spending money in the shops, the pubs, the restaurants. It was very hard.'

His cancer, meanwhile, showed no signs of retreating. The chemotherapy wasn't working and in a final throw of the dice, his consultant said he could try an experimental oral treatment. A few tablets a day, along with monthly blood tests and scans are all that's needed and it seems to be working. The cancer has been kept at bay and he's feeling fitter and healthier than he has done in a long time.

The banks are still hovering in the background though and Ian is looking to sell up, 'for the right price'. He doesn't want the lodge to be let go or run into the ground. He still believes in its potential as a salmon fishery, still believes it has a future.

'I would love to see it come back to be able to provide a contribution locally and I would love to see it continue in the same vein. Now whether that will be possible if it's a fishing lodge, or whether it's going to be as holiday homes or maybe self-catering units allied to the lodge, or people locally taking them and using them for self-catering, I don't know.'

No regrets, though. No looking back in anger, only fond memories.

'There's no point worrying about the things you can't change, and you can't change what's gone on. It was great fun. I sit down with a couple of the ghillies that live locally now and we have a beer and we talk about the great times that went on here because it was such fun. You certainly couldn't regret it, but you would love to see it come back, back to providing employment, revenue for people, and bring it back to the point that I had it. To see it come back to something approaching that would be very satisfying from my point of view because I don't ever want to see it just falling to rack and ruin and not be used.'

Dreams sometimes come true, but oftentimes they don't. You think you have it in your hands, but then it just slips away down the river. We open another beer and sit in silence. The fishing records lie open before us, glimpses into a golden past. Have I lived too much in the past, I wonder as I sip my beer, part of the reason for my restlessness and angst, looking back at what might have been rather than cherishing what's around me in the here and now? It's probably why, throughout my year of journeying, I have been drawn to the dreamers, people who wanted to live life based on a passion that wouldn't go away or be given up. I want that one thing they all had that gave them a focus for living.

Singularity of purpose is the phrase that runs through my mind as I look across the quiet fields that run down to the river and I hear Rudyard Kipling's words echo in my head:

> If you can dream – and not make dreams your master;
> If you can think – and not make thoughts your aim;
> If you can meet with Triumph and Disaster
> And treat those two impostors just the same;

Haunted by Waters

It's not all happy endings either, I realise, but if you can look back at the good times and the bad and see that both sides of the experience were worth it, then you can be content with the memories you live with now. At the end of this season, this year of trying, I do feel content – the angst, restlessness and stress having abated. It has been a year of experience and truly seeing what matters in life.

The memories are all around us in the old lodge. On the walls, in the rooms, in the silence. But time doesn't stand still and the Blackwater River still flows on in the fields below. There once was a salmon fishery here, and before that there was a railway station. There was always the river, though. And the salmon. That's what lingers in the passing.

12.
Lockdowns in Time

*I*t was only five weeks to Christmas, the kids counting down the days. 'Let's get to December before we start the Christmas songs,' I plead with them, unsuccessfully. The tree and Advent calendar would wait until then at least, I say, drowned out by a chorus of 'Jingle Bells' from the back of the car.

It was mid-November and we were driving to Salthill on the outskirts of Galway to the Irish fly fishing fair. Little did we know it would be our last fly fishing outing for a long time to come. It had become a ritual of sorts for me and the kids, a day marked in our calendars weeks in advance, a day spent together having fishing-related fun. It was how we closed the fishing year before Santa and presents became the main focus.

We had a three-hour drive ahead of us and the backpack on the seat beside me was full with popcorn, smoothies, fruit, treats and water. Ryan and Charlie had packed their own goodies – the Nintendo Switch, Lego, notebooks and pens – half of the adventure would be the car journey itself. I remember when I first went to the fair on my own and used it for some welcome fly fishing time in the off-season. It usually takes place near my own birthday and was also a great opportunity to pick up some fly fishing books as a present to myself. Now I had my own two sons accompanying me. It's a special time together and gives me so much joy to be able to pass on my love of fishing and the outdoors to them. I relish the solitary nature of fishing but have an image in my mind of my kids as grown adults coming back to Tipperary to visit, grabbing their rods and bags from their room and taking me out fishing. Sharing the sport with them in years to come will be just as special.

The entrance hall to the hotel was packed when we arrived mid-morning, mainly with men carrying shopping bags of fly fishing paraphernalia from stall to stall. There were tackle dealers; stalls with salmon flies, trout flies, pike flies; there were book sellers, talks and casting demos; and most popular of all with the crowd were the fly-tying stands where some of the most renowned fly-tyers from around the world sat at their desks tying for everyone to see.

I haven't had the interest or time to practise tying my own flies (yet) and many anglers will say that it's only when you've caught a fish on a fly you've tied yourself that your fly fishing journey is complete. The boys are very artistic and are fascinated to see how thread and feathers are wound and bound around a hook to create an artificial depiction of something that will fool a fish. It's an art as old as the sport itself and many of the most famous fly-tyers nowadays create works meant for frames and hanging on the wall, aesthetic pieces to be admired, not fished with. As we gaze at each of the different creations in front of us I can see the boys' eyes light up in wonder at the colours and feathers all brought together in this way. They have a go themselves and I promise we'll have a go at home as well.

The day ends with chicken and chips and one final walk around the fair before a run on the small beach that lies across the road on the Salthill promenade. Last year you could have

Haunted by Waters

worn shorts and a t-shirt with the warmth of the sun but this year it was more like a typical November, with icy-cold wind and sleety rain. The beach trip ends with Ryan and Charlie getting a soaking from the spray of an incoming wave against the rocks, which made them howl in delight, but now it's definitely time for us to head home.

We would be back just as it was getting dark. Another year over, another season behind me and the boys would have their memory of us marking the tradition of the fair.

This time, as I drove down the motorway for home, I wasn't feeling melancholy at the closing of the year, I was instead upbeat and contented. I had been on a year-long experience discovering the countryside and something about myself, finding fulfilment in the journey, for once not trying to squeeze and hold onto the days, but just enjoying them as they played out, happy to be there in the first place. Life unfolds in unexpected ways and making it happen and then letting it play out has given a new depth and meaning to it all. I glanced in the mirror, my boys asleep in the back of the car, and revelled in the silence all around me while I watched the hills and land spotlighted by the setting sun as we passed further south. I hope I have given my boys something to remember me by in future decades, I think to myself, as well as a sense of place and an appreciation of nature.

As we pull up to the house, I can see the lights are on. The boys stretch and stir, their hands still resting on their bags of newly bought lures and flies. As we gather up our things they both ask, 'Dad, can we tie a fly before dinner?' and my heart swells with pride.

Who would have believed however that the flies I helped them tie that evening on the dinner table would be left in their box gathering dust for the months to follow? We innocently celebrated Christmas and the New Year making plans for the start of a new decade, not knowing what was silently spreading around the world, ultimately affecting us all. With frosted grass to welcome in the mornings and log fires from late afternoon on, it seemed like any other December.

Then when the lockdown happened we were all so unprepared. Life just stopped. One minute you're reading about a virus far off in China, the next you're being told the schools are closed, shops are shut and you have to stay at home.

When it happened in Ireland in the middle of March I had still to wet a line in 2020 and I looked back at all the missed opportunities from 1 January to 17 March. How many chances had I missed to be out with rod and line on the water and never bothered? Rain and floods knocked most plans on the head earlier in the year, but still.

There were salmon being caught on the Drowes in high water and while the opening of the Blackwater on 1 February was a bit of a washout, there was also the odd fish being caught. What I wouldn't have given to have those chances all over again.

Just to be standing in the river, feeling the flowing waters pushing against my waders, the same flow anchoring and taking my fly downstream in the expectant hope of a take. This should have been the highlight reel for my year so far.

Thankfully, though, before the government announcement of the 2-km lockdown, I still had time to fill out and collect my 2020 membership for my local fly fishing club. Even if I couldn't travel to Connemara, Kerry or Cork, my local water wouldn't be out of reach at some point in the future, I hoped.

By the time I had called to the club secretary's house to hand over my fee in return for the coveted membership card, lockdowns in Europe had already begun. That same day all the school children in Ireland had also been sent home. Suddenly the coronavirus was becoming much more real.

I didn't stay long in the secretary's house and made a point of saying goodbye on a positive note with 'I'll see you on the river when we can make it.' The virus and what might happen was all we could talk about in those few minutes, with Kevin telling me of the panic buying of toilet rolls and hand sanitiser in the retail warehouse where he worked. But at least I had the membership card now safely in my possession.

That evening at home I opened up Google Maps and plotted the travel distance from my house to the river. Yes, it was under 2 km, the maximum permitted distance one could travel. Could I or should I go?

Once a week I would drive in the evening to the supermarket in the local town, but there were few cars or people around, with almost everywhere closed up. Darkness and despondency had set in. The streets had an eerie quietness and stillness to them. The pandemic was part of all of our lives now.

It was very tempting to know that I could just head down to the Suir with little chance of meeting anyone else, and even better, the river and fish being largely undisturbed. With the world gone silent, I could fish blissfully on in my own little bubble.

But it didn't feel right. We were all suffering together, a sense of fear and uncertainty about the world and society hanging over it all. It wasn't a cloud of despair, but it was a shadow of doubt and questioning.

I wasn't the only one who felt this way. When I spoke to Tom Doc Sullivan, the Lough Corrib guide who lives by the lakeshore, to find out if he had been doing any fishing, he said he hadn't wanted to go out either. 'It didn't feel right,' he repeated to me. It wasn't the morals, the ethics or the regulations, it was something more.

I would wait; I would hunker down with my family like everyone else and see the storm out. Fishing would be there when we came through it eventually. From the other anglers I spoke to, it seemed to be the same mindset amongst them all. The time would come again, but just not now.

In lockdown and stuck at home just as the fly fishing season opened in March on my local river was a depressing and incomprehensible time. One minute you're busy making plans, the next … well, the next minute you're just not. You're being forced to take a step back. And maybe sometimes that's not such a bad thing.

In the context of what had gone on, fishing seemed both totally irrelevant and more important than ever before; it served as a benchmark, a reminder of how life truly had changed. So we got on with it, figured out how to divide childcare and working from home, while trying to keep up some sort of routine to stay sane. News of the Covid deaths each evening was a stark reminder of what it was all about. Days became weeks and weeks became months. We were winning the battle, we were told, the social distancing and lockdowns were working. There were even the tentative signs of society reopening. Did I dare think about fishing again?

The first inkling I had was an email from my local fly fishing shop.

Mayfly time! Get your new gear for the mayfly season!

I had to check my phone for the date. Yes, it really was the middle of May. Normally trips would have been planned and booked weeks, if not months, in advance for this time of the year. Mayfly on the Corrib and the rest of the western lakes as well as other special places was always set in stone in the fly fishing calendar for so many anglers.

For me, if I could make a trip to Corrib at least once a year, it meant I was observing the holy sacrament. This year, however, there was to be no trip across the Shannon or west into Connemara.

I *could* go fishing on the Suir, though. Travel restrictions had been eased by now and people were starting to venture out a little more. Fishing was permissible and after more than two months of lockdown it felt okay to be going out to the river again.

Other anglers were sharing pictures on Instagram of decent-sized trout being caught and it was becoming harder to resist. When the email announcing mayfly time arrived in my inbox, I mulled it over for a few days.

We had been blessed with the weather as well since the lockdown began. There had been little or no rain, the kids were able to play outside in the garden, taking some of the pressure off home life.

Evening times especially could be bliss. Balmy heat without a hint of a breeze, you could almost pretend you were away on holidays. It was getting increasingly hard to just stay at home now.

I hadn't fixed a day to go back to the river but that Friday evening, after a busy week, I didn't want to be sitting at home anymore. It was just after 9 p.m., all was quiet, the kids were in bed asleep and my wife was upstairs reading.

I opened my fishing closet where my rods, bags, reels, jackets and fly boxes are all stored, ready to be taken out at a moment's notice. There was my #3–4 weight trout rod alongside my sling bag with tippet, leaders and flies, waiting in the corner, as if to say, '*Finally* ... what took you so long?'

I checked the car dashboard as I pulled away from the house: 21.10. 'I'll be fishing by 21.20,' I thought, with a smile on my face. I didn't know what to expect as I drove down the country road. Would it be full of other like-minded anglers? Or would I be the only one?

There were two cars there already and two anglers by the water's edge, chatting. Then one of the anglers said his goodbyes to his friend and started heading upstream looking for some likely risers – just what I was planning on doing. The great thing about this beat is that there are so many stretches where you can slip in quietly without annoying others.

Standing by my car, I threaded my line through the rod rings, joined the fine-tapered leader via its loop-to-loop connection and tied on some 6x tippet before finally threading the single dry fly which I would use as a searching pattern on the water.

I hooked the fly onto the keeper ring, checked my sling bag and pockets again: everything was where it should be. I clicked the doors of the car shut and placed the keys in my bag. I took a deep breath and smiled to myself. It felt good to be out again.

As I clambered across the plank that led over the ditch and into the fields, I could hear the murmurings of the river making its way over the rocks. The familiar fields of Ballybrado were lush green, wildflowers appearing here and there in pockets. There was no sign of the usual sheep and all was quiet except for the birds and the running water.

I stopped for a moment as I always do to read the sign at the bridge erected in honour of the Irish fishery reformer William Joshua Ffennell who was born at Ballybrado, the nearby house on the hill.

It's nice to be reminded that two hundred years ago in these same fields, people were fishing and looking out for the future of wild fish. How many pandemics and plagues had they also seen in those intervening years, I wondered. The last few weeks of our lives had been just a drop in the ocean of the world; it was our generation's turn to deal with a pandemic. Many more people had dealt with one before and it was just our time to face up to it now.

I walked on. There was the weir and the water still flowing steadily, while upstream the swans made their way discreetly along the far bank. It was all as it should be.

The other angler was making his way further ahead so I decided to leave the uppermost stretches to him. Just above the weir would suit me fine, where there was a long, slow glide and plenty of spots in between the reeds to cast a willing fly.

The trout were rising sporadically, though there wasn't much by way of flies hatching. There seemed to be occasional pale watery duns and olives flittering around me and then as the evening drew in, the hatch became more incessant.

It was all a welcome sight, a return to normal. Despite it all, nature was still keeping to her habits. My first casts were rusty as I struggled to get out enough line to land clean and true but still the trout rose and finally I was casting smoothly again.

Same result, though, the trout were blissfully ignoring the flies I was trying to tempt them with. I would see a rise, cast just above it and watch as the fly passed by untouched. Seconds later the trout would rise again just where my fly had passed. It was maddening and oh so familiar and I couldn't help but smile as the time passed and soon dusk fell upon me.

The dusk then turned into darkness. I had tried different parts of the pool but with the same result and now I could feel I was merely going through the motions. I was barely able to see the fly and so I reeled in before clambering back up the bank.

I sat there in the gloam frustrated at my lack of success and obvious rustiness, but happy, listening to the running water. There wasn't a soul around, it was just me and the river. It was time to head home and I walked back through the fields towards my car with a contentment I hadn't felt in a long time. Just to be out, here, by the river, it almost seemed as if the world was returning to its right path.

By the time I arrived home and opened the front door, my wife was getting ready to go to bed.

'Have a good time?' she asked, stifling a yawn. 'Catch any fish?'

'Yes … and no,' I replied with a smile. 'But it's good to be back.'

Acknowledgements

I have always been fascinated by history and the rural landscape, like you're walking in the footsteps of the past and continuing on that journey. This book started out as a desire to get out and fish more, to travel the country and experience the different facets of Irish fly fishing culture, from the people to the places.

But my travels were about more than just the external, more than just the sights and sounds. It also became a journey inward as the time spent outdoors, surrounded by nature, made me stop and reconsider what was important in life. This was all pre-pandemic of course but the same themes and issues merely became more amplified and highlighted during the lockdowns.

Little did I realise, however, that my year travelling to the lakes and rivers around Ireland would become a book. Until one evening when I felt the urge to sit down and write, to try and put into words what it all meant and to try and capture some essence of what Irish fly fishing culture is all about.

One evening became two, became three, became weeks and months. I soon realised that the same commitment I had made to fish more was translating now into a daily commitment to put it into words and before I knew it, I had enough written for a book.

Fly fishing is a niche sport however and when I felt brave enough to send a draft to Ciara Doorley at Hachette, I was blown away by her enthusiastic response to it. It was about much more than fly fishing, she told me, and her positivity, guidance and encouragement throughout has been an absolute pleasure as we worked on getting it ready for publication. Ciara, for your belief in what my journey could bring to the wider reading public, my sincerest thanks.

To Susan McKeever, whose tireless work on the manuscript improved it in so many ways – despite many a head scratching about fly fishing terms, I'm sure! – thank you.

Thanks also to Joanna Smyth for your help with the permissions and proofs and to Elaine and the Hachette PR team. Sincere thanks as well to Aonghus Meaney for his detailed work on tidying up the text.

To Paula McGloin, my heart lifted when Ciara sent me the book cover design. It captured perfectly the journey, the landscape, the experience of it all. Thank you for an incredible illustration.

To the guides, fishery managers and lodge owners whom I met and spoke to, your time, insights and assistance were invaluable and your stories inspiring. You opened a window into your lives and helped capture what fly fishing in Ireland is all about and why you do it.

My utmost thanks to: Shane Gallagher, Glenda Powell, Tom Doc Sullivan, Peter Mantle, Ken Whelan, David Norman, Des Chew, Noel Carr, Michael Wade, Ian Powell and Neil O'Shea.

In remembrance also of Peter O'Reilly, one of the country's finest fly anglers and who helped bring the sport to a wider audience through his incomparable books and tireless work.

To all the fly anglers I have met beside the water and am yet to meet, we fish on in hope despite the changing conditions and an uncertain future. This book is only a snapshot into the waters that can be fished in Ireland and I look forward to many more journeys and experiences to come.

Thanks also to my local club, the Cahir and District Anglers Association, and Kevin Rowe; to Inland Fisheries Ireland for their help and for keeping anglers regularly informed of latest reports and catches. Their weekly newsletter is an invaluable resource.

A special word of thanks as well to Paddy Bushe for his time, and for permission to use his translation of *The Song of Amergin*. Whilst not an angler, Paddy opened my eyes to just how intertwined our history and our writings are with the lakes and rivers of our countryside.

To Trina, my love and thanks as always for your unwavering belief and support in what my heart wants and yearns for. It was you who encouraged me to pursue my 'own piece of heaven' whenever I could and without you I wouldn't have done it.

To Ryan and Charlie, my fishing buddies, whose awe at capturing their first fish will never leave me and is a reminder of what it's all about and why we should never get too caught up in the small stuff.

And to Gloria, I can't wait to bring you with me to the water's edge and introduce you to the magic of what fly fishing has brought to my life, but yet which still pales in comparison to the joy you have brought to us all since your arrival into our lives.